P9-DEP-234

PRAGUE
ART AND HISTORY

TIM PORTER

FLOW EAST

© 1995 Flow East Limited, Mostecká 12, 118 00 Prague 1
© Text 1991 Tim Porter

General Coordinator
Nathalie Shashou

Photographs
Jiří Macht, Gordon Hardwick

Research
Alexandra Miksánkova

Assistance given by
Ministry of Trade and Tourism,
National Gallery,
National Museum in Prague,
President's Cultural Office - Aura Pont

ISBN 88-901108-8-0

Produced by Summerfield Press, Florence
Printed in Italy by Faenza Industrie Grafiche

CONTENTS

7 Message from President Havel

9 Introduction

10 Map of the city

13 Staré Město - The Old City

53 Malá Strana

67 The Castle

91 Hradčany and Nový Svět

103 Josefov - The Prague Ghetto

111 Nové Město - The New City

122 Chronology

126 Useful information

In 1464 the Czech King George of Poděbrady sent an important message to the King of France, Louis XI, suggesting that he should form and lead a peaceful league of Christian kings, a defensive association based on the observation of international rights to prevent warfare between the member states and to guarantee their defence. In my opinion it was not by accident that one of the first serious attempts to create a peaceful Europe should have originated in Central Europe. Historically this region has always been the focus of European conflicts and it is therefore understandable that it should show a strong interest in peace and security for Europe as a whole.

In our country we have freedom of opinion and belief: for the first time since World War II all Catholic dioceses are headed by a bishop and the monastic orders are active again. Our state has no state ideology. The only idea that inspires our internal and international policies is an idea based on the respect of human rights in general and of the uniqueness of each individual human being.

We feel that we are a sovereign state and we want to live in friendship with all nations all over the world.

VÁCLAV HAVEL
President of the ČSFR

From a speech delivered before the European Parliament at Strasbourg, 10 May 1990. This extract is quoted with the kind permission of the President's Office in Prague.

INTRODUCTION

Prague is a city of the unexpected. Rich in mythology, one only has to stand in the middle of Charles Bridge at dead of night amongst the moon shadows cast by the early Gothic bridge towers and Baroque statues to appreciate something of the special atmosphere of the place. Despite her turbulent history, which has seen her placed on more than one occasion at the burning edge of ideological frictions, Prague has emerged with the main fabric of her architectural wealth intact. From Malá Strana, with its cobbled squares lined with the Baroque palaces of the illustrious elite, through the tortuous meanderings of the alleys flowing amongst the Gothic market squares of Staroměstske, to the looming shadows of Hradčany Castle that raises St. Vitus skyward like a chalice held aloft to the heavens, there is always something of interest close at hand. As the swans glide past on the wide waters of the Vltava, over the rippling reflections of turrets and domes, or skeins of mist drape themselves between her seven hills to be punctured by spires and steeples, Prague challenges us to know the unknowable.

1. Strahovský klášter — *Strahov Monastery*
2. Loreta — *Loreto*
3. Růžový sad — *Rose Gardens*
4. Pražský hrad + Katedrála Sv. Vita — *Castle + Cathedral of St. Vitus*
5. Sv. Mikuláše — *St. Nicolas Church*
6. Pražské Jezulátko — *Infant Jesus of Prague*
7. Belveder — *Belvedere*
8. Hanavský pavilón — *Hanavsky Pavilion*
9. Dům umělců — *House of the Artists*
10. Staronová synagoga — *Old New Synagogue*
11. Anežský klášter — *St. Agnes Monastery*
12. Karlův Most — *Charles Bridge*
13. Staroměstská radnice — *Old Town Hall*
14. Týnský chrám — *Our Lady before Tyn*
15. Prašná brána — *Powder Tower*
16. Lidový dům — *The People's House*
17. Karolinum — *Carolinum*
18. Tylovo divadlo — *Tyl Theater*
19. Betlémská kaple — *Bethlehem Chapel*
20. Národní divadlo — *National Theater*
21. Novoměstská radnice — *New Town Hall*
22. Národní muzeun — *National Museum*
23. Pod. Emauzy — *Emauzy Church*

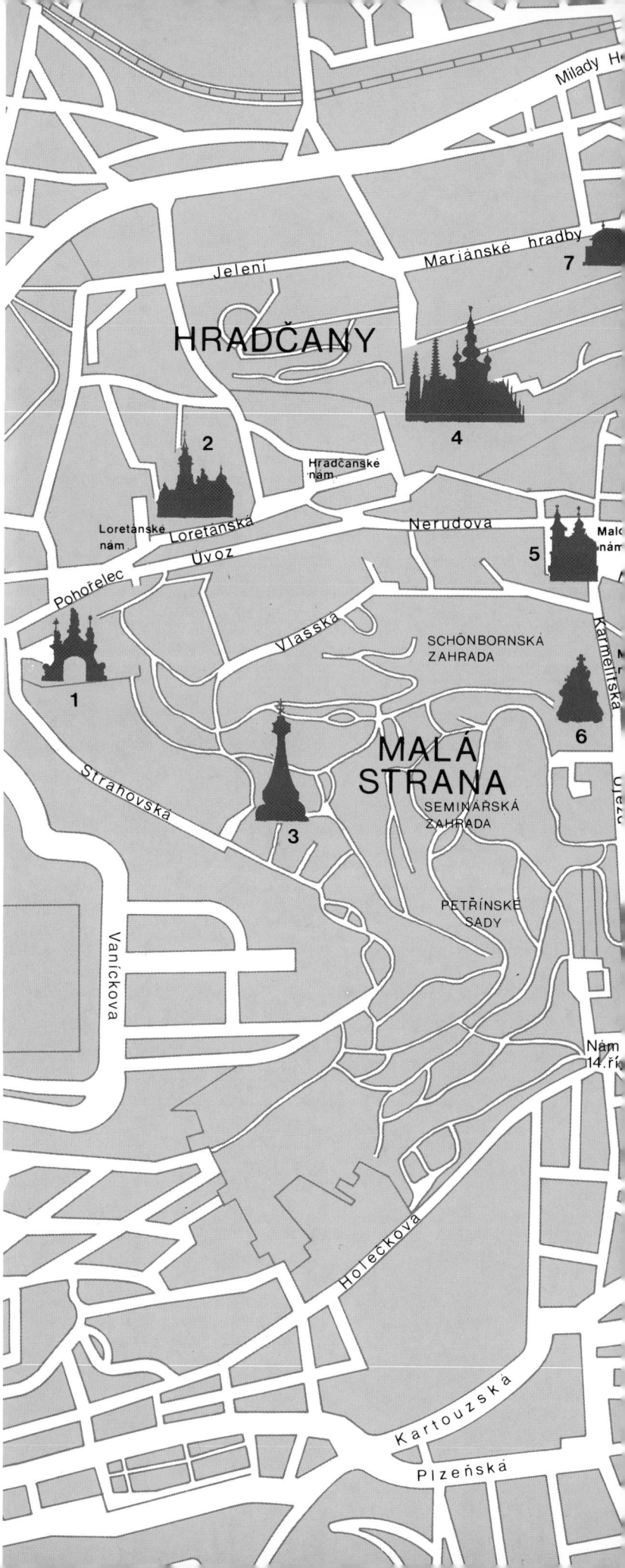

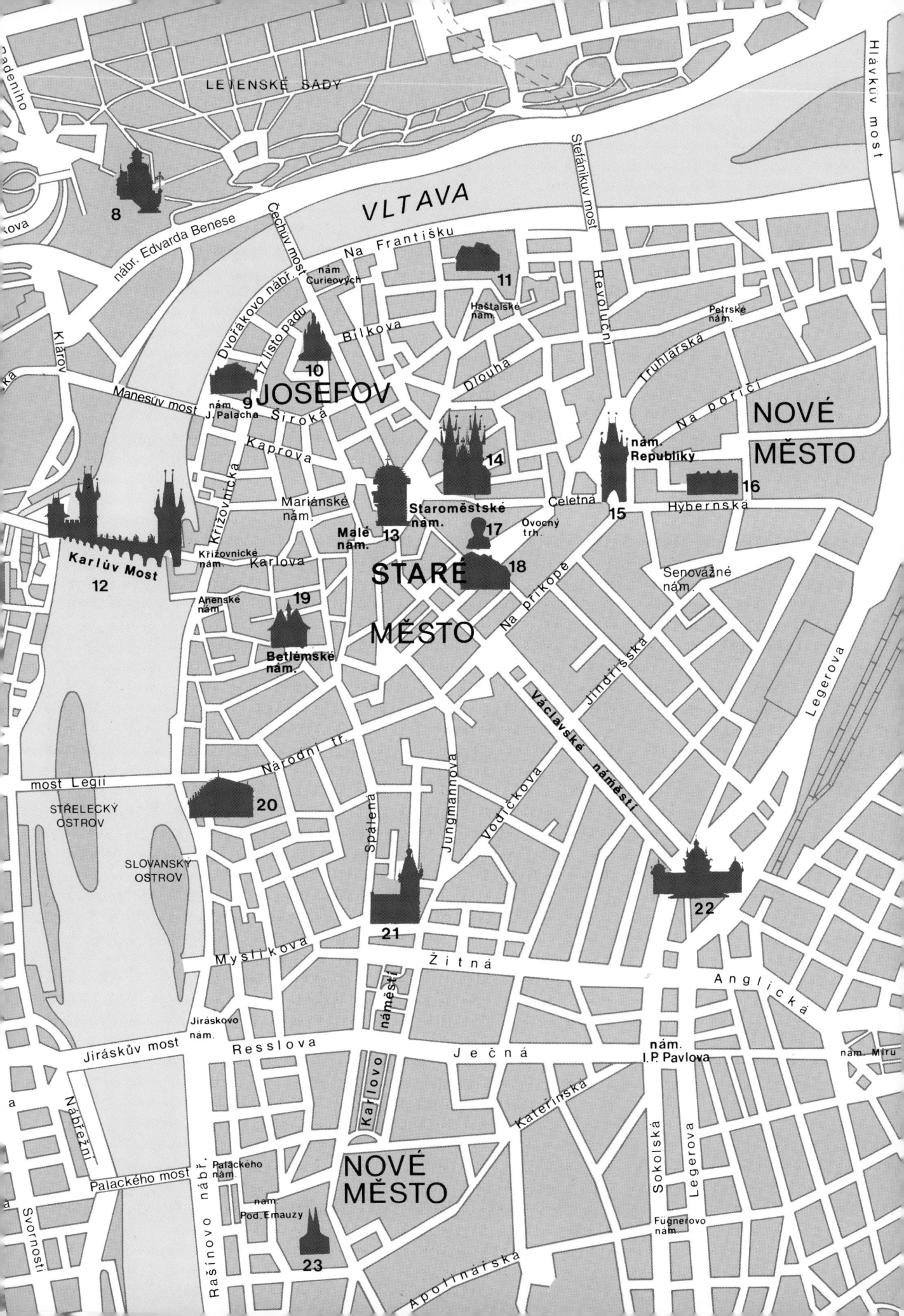
LETENSKÉ SADY
VLTAVA
Hlávkův most
Štefánikův most
Čechův most
nábř. Edvarda Beneše
Na Františku
nám. Curieových
Dvořákovo nábř.
17. listopadu
Bílkova
Haštalské nám.
Revoluční
Petrské nám.
Truhlářská
Klárov
Manesův most
nám. J. Palacha
JOSEFOV
Široká
Dlouhá
Na poříčí
NOVÉ MĚSTO
Kaprova
nám. Republiky
Křižovnická
Mariánské nám.
Staroměstské nám.
Celetná
Hybernská
Malé nám.
Ovocný trh.
Karlův Most
Křižovnické nám.
Karlova
STARÉ MĚSTO
Senovážné nám.
Anenské nám.
Na příkopě
Betlémské nám.
Jindřišská
Legerova
Václavské náměstí
Národní tř.
most Legií
STŘELECKÝ OSTROV
Spálená
Jungmannova
Vodičkova
SLOVANSKÝ OSTROV
Myslíkova
Žitná
Anglická
Jiráskovo nám.
Jiráskův most
Resslova
Ječná
nám. I.P. Pavlova
nám. Míru
Karlovo náměstí
Nábřežní
Palackého most
Palackého nám.
Kateřinská
Sokolská
Legerova
NOVÉ MĚSTO
nám. Pod. Emauzy
Svornosti
Rašínovo nábř.
Fügnerovo nám.
Apotékářská
8
9
10
11
12
13
14
15
16
17
18
19
20
21
22
23

Charles Bridge at night.

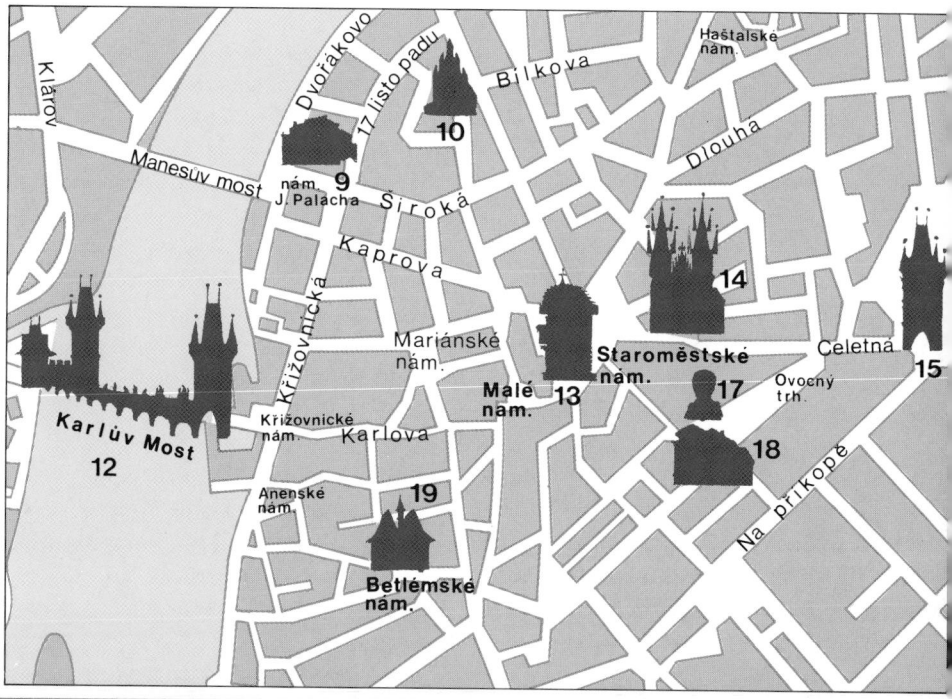

STARÉ MĚSTO - THE OLD TOWN

'he area now known as the Old Town was the centre of omanesque Prague. Here, where the road joining Prague Castle with 'yšehrad intersected the ancient east-west trade route, there grew up n important commercial centre, on a site close to the present Old 'own Square. The merchants who settled here in the twelfth century ood to profit not only from international trade but also from the ommerce in luxury goods to service the requirements of the royal ourts. At this early stage the settlement was not yet a town in the edieval sense of the word as it possessed no town charter and, erhaps more importantly for the security of the inhabitants, no own walls.

Vith the accession of Wenceslas I in 1230 a charter recognizing the ights of the inhabitants was finally granted and the area now borded y the streets Národní, Na Příkopě and Revoluční was surrounded by double wall and a moat. The name of the street Na Příkopě iterally "on the moat") is a modern reminder of these ancient ortifications. Preserved in the foyer of the Můstek underground tation are the remains of the original stone bridge that spanned the oat. This stretch of walls was further fortified by thirteen towers nd gateways, none of which unfortunately have survived, although heir location is recalled by the thirteen streets which enter the Old 'own from the main thoroughfares mentioned above.

'he **Powder Tower** (Prašná Brána) still stands on the western side of Náměstí Republiky at the entrance to the medieval street Celetná. Driginally a late Gothic tower, dating from the end of the fifteenth entury, it stands on the site of one of the earlier gateways in honour f the newly elected King Vladislav Jagiello (1471-1516), a member f the Polish royal family. Financed by the inhabitants of the Old 'own, work started in 1475 though four hundred years were to lapse before its completion. In 1484 the builders laid down their ools when Vladislav transferred his residence from the neighbouring Royal Court to Prague Castle, a move prompted by increasingly olatile relations between the townspeople and the patriciate who vere attempting to reintroduce Catholicism. The uncompleted tower vas furnished with a temporary roof and served as a store for unpowder until the end of the seventeenth century giving us the ame by which it is known today. It is easy to be fooled by the urist Neo-Gothic reconstructions carried out in Prague by Josef Mocker in the late nineteenth century and the Powder Tower is no xception. Although the ornamental decoration of Matěj Rejsek, Prague's principal late Gothic architect alongside Benedikt Ried, is

Page 6
The Old Town from the roof of the National Theatre.

Page 8
The Gothic taste for sculptural ornament is very much in evidence on the Powder Tower.

still very much in evidence, much of the present character of the tower, including the hip roof, is the result of Mocker's work, necessitated largely by the damage incurred during the Prussian siege of the city in 1737.

Adjoining the tower to the right is the unmistakable Secessionist splendour of the **People's House** (Obecní Dům). Until 1679 the site was occupied by the buildings of the Royal Court (although they ceased to function as such in 1484). These were severely damaged by the fire that ravaged the Old Town in the same year; after it was rebuilt the complex housed an archiepiscopal seminary and later a barracks and school for cadets. The present building was erected between 1906 and 1912 at a time when Czech artists and architects were held in the thrall of the anti-historical style of Art Nouveau, which took its decorative motifs not from the well-thumbed vocabulary of historical antecedents, but from the mother of all invention, Nature herself.

Enter the Old Town via Celetná, one of the oldest streets in Prague and you join what is undoubtedly the main promenade of the city. Suddenly everyone seems to be going in the same direction, following not only the ancient east-west trade route but also that of the coronation procession, which cut a swathe through the mostly circuitous medieval streets on its way from the Royal Court to St. Vitus Cathedral. Every inch of the journey is steeped in history, some of its moments more glorious than others. Prague still has many well-kept secrets. The cores of Gothic and Renaissance buildings lie hidden behind the doors of some of the houses, their earlier ancestry belied by subsequent Baroque and Neo-Classical accretions. Two such buildings are the high Baroque palaces of **Hrzán** and **Buquoy**. If you look hard enough though, some benign power has afforded us glimpses into the more distant past. In the gateway of number 17, **Menhart House**, for example, we can still see a small bricked-up portal from the fourteenth century. Look high up on the facade of number 13, **Caretto Millesimo Palace**, and you will see two brick-built Gothic side gables.

But for those gasps of wonder that only an unexpected confrontation with the ancient past can procure we have to venture underground. Towards the end of the thirteenth century the frequent flooding of the Vltava had proved such a nuisance that it was decided to raise the ground level of the whole Old Town by two to three metres. This, together with the building boom generated by the new urban rights at the time of Wenceslas I and a devastating fire in 1291, meant that Gothic Prague grew up literally on top of its Romanesque predecessor, swallowing the ground floors of the old stone houses whole and consigning them to a clandestine life beneath the new street level. These two facts, the preponderance of stone built architecture and the artificial raising of the ground level, reflect the ever increasing prosperity of the Old Town. Many of these basements have only relatively recently been discovered and now serve as restaurants and clubs, such as **U zlatého jelena** (The Golden Stag) or **U Sixtu** (At the House of Sixth, No. 2), both in Celetná. The most important of these subterranean time capsules, however, is the originally Romanesque **Palace of George of Poděbrady** in

The Secessionist splendour of the People's House.

ZDAR TOBĚ PRAHO VZDORU JEŽ TU TOBĚ
JAK ODOLÁVAT VĚKY BOUŘÍM VĚNU

The Old Town Square.

Řetězová. Without doubt the largest of the Romanesque structures preserved in the cellarage of the Old Town, the palace, with its vaulting springing from central piers, provides a clear idea of the layout and construction techniques employed in the domestic stone architecture of the day.

The effect of leaving Celetná and entering the majestic space of the **Old Town Square** is somewhat akin to what a log must feel having ridden white waters to be jettisoned from an estuary mouth into the still expanse of the ocean. Yet its beauty and noble proportions belie some of the grim moments from the city's history. In 1422 the square provided the backdrop for the execution of Jan Želivský, a Hussite radical responsible for inciting his fellows during the first Prague defenestration in 1419, thereby provoking the Hussite wars. Sixteen years later it was the scene for Hussite reprisals on a wider scale when Jan Roháč of Dubé was put to death along with 56 of his comrades. In 1621 the twenty-seven leaders of the Protestant anti-Habsburg uprising were executed as a final and dramatic warning that all attempts to resist the monarchical autocracy and the reintroduction of Catholicism were doomed to failure.

All the major streets that enter the Old Town are drawn inexorably

owards this the ancient commercial epicentre like the individual lken threads of a mighty web. The first markets in the area were ctually held in the **Týn Ungelt**, a walled trading centre dating from 135 and situated between the churches of Our Lady before Týn and t. James. At this time the largest market contained within the Old 'own walls was in the Gall Town. This initially autonomous ettlement was founded in 1232 and granted a royal charter around 234 as part of Wenceslas I's progressive programme of urbanization. 'he rights and privileges of the two towns were unified in 1287; at bout the same time the craftsmen were organizing themselves into a rotherhood which in due course became a guild. The growth of rade at the end of the thirteenth century led to the setting up of pecialized market places and to the codification of the rights and uties of foreign merchants at a time when life in the Old Town was entred around four main squares; Staroměstské (Old Town), Iavelské (Gall Town), Kozí (The Goat) and Mariánské (The Virgin Iary). There was still no real form of self administration, however, he reins being held by the Royal Magistrate directly appointed by nd responsible to the King. In 1296 the Prague patriciate, who had rown wealthy from trading in silver extracted from the mines at

The Old Town Hall Tower affords a superb view across the Old Town.

St. James Church: Baroque ornamental sculpture above the left door.

Kutná Hora, petitioned Wenceslas II for permission to build a town hall and appoint a town clerk. The King, eager to maintain a direct hold on the affairs of the Old Town, approved only the appointment of the clerk. The boot was on the other foot, however, when Wenceslas, keen to raise the international status of Prague, sought support from the baronial Estates to found a university. The barons, realizing that it was legal studies in France and Italy which provided ambitious monarchs with the necessary arguments and expertise to construct a more centralized rule, successfully frustrated his plans. The townspeople had to wait until 1338 for the right to build their own town hall. This was finally granted by John of Luxemburg in return for their financing of his adventurous foreign exploits. This town hall, which is really an agglomeration of buildings purchased and adapted over a period of time, is now the focus of the Old Town Square, not least because of the renowned **Astronomical Clock** set in the western facade of the tower. The clock in its earliest form dates from about 1410 and is attributed to Mikuláš of Kadaň. A morbid legend relates how Wenceslas IV (1378-1419) had him blinded so that the remarkable feat of engineering should never be repeated. Although it is not true, the mere fact that such a story

The renowned Astronomical Clock.

The characteristic, multi-turreted towers of the Church of Our Lady before Týn echo those of the Old Town Hall.

should be invented is a reflection of the low esteem in which Wenceslas IV was held by the populace, but then he did have the misfortune of acceding to the position held by his glorious father, the Holy Roman Emperor Charles IV. He was not, by the way, the Good King Wenceslas of British Christmas tradition: it was St. Wenceslas, made Duke of Bohemia in 921, who had earned himself this term of endearment. The function of the clock was perfected in 1490 by Hanuš of Růže and displays just about everything regarding time and its relationship with the Heavens that you should ever need to know.

The upper face is split into four main zones, the blue referring to day, the black to night and the two brown areas to dawn and dusk. The outer ring bears the twenty-four hour clock of normal Czech usage, the inner the anti-meridian and post-meridian in Roman numerals. The smaller inset face displays the signs of the zodiac and the respective positions of the Sun, Moon and Pole Star. The lower calendar face, a copy of the one executed by Josef Mánes in 1866 (the original now resides in the entrance hall of the Municipal Museum), is decorated with beautiful allegorical paintings of the months of the year. Around its edge are displayed the names of all the Saints for every day of the year. On the hour, every hour until ten in the evening, the crowds gather like disciples round a prophet to witness the ritualistic dance of the figures next to the main clock

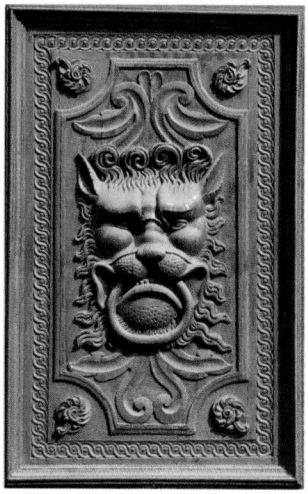

Old Town Hall - the Renaissance window.

Ornamental door in the Old Town.

"Praga - Caput - Regni."

Renaissance sgraffito decoration on the House at the Minute.

Clam Gallas Palace.

Štorch's House.

face and receive solemn benediction from the twelve apostles as they file past the two door openings at the top. As the figure of Death tolls his knell, the Turk on his left shakes his head denying that his time is up. The Turk was a popular subject of loathing at a time when the Ottoman Empire had expanded to include the lowlands of Hungary, thereby constituting a very real threat to the Czech domains. On the other side meanwhile, the miser feebly shakes his stick and bag of gold as the vain man admires his reflection in the looking glass.

Most of the interior of the Old Town Hall is only accessible by joining one of the guided tours that depart from the foyer on the

The richly decorated façade of Rott's House.

hour, after the striking of the clock. Situated next to the clock tower is the main entrance portal, where once more we can discern the hand of Matěj Rejsek in the intricate carving of figures and flora on the frame. The ornamental decoration of doorways became a prominent feature of Prague architectural embellishment, and so many of the entrances to palaces are guarded by monumental figural sculpture that it is a wonder the night air is not filled with their stone groans. Further along to the left is the beautiful **House at the Minute**, one of the most recent buildings acquired for use as part of the Town Hall in 1886. Originally a Gothic structure, it was rebuilt during the Renaissance when it received its sgraffito decoration,

Nineteenth-century painted decoration in Myslíkova.

Right
The majestic spires of the Church of Our Lady before Týn rise up behind the Týn School and the House at the White Unicorn.

portraying classical and biblical scenes as well as allegorical figures of the Virtues. The pictorial decoration of building facades is another characteristic feature of Prague which, although frowned on by the intellectualizing of the Baroque, came back into vogue with Art Nouveau at the end of the nineteenth and beginning of the twentieth centuries. There are two fine examples in the vicinity of the Old Town Square; one at **Štorch's House** (No.16) and the other in the Malé Náměstí at **Rott's House** (No.3). In the fifteenth century a printing press was located here which produced the first Bible in the Czech language in 1488.

The top of the clock tower affords a remarkable view of the whole of the Old Town. From here the meandering network of medieval streets reveals how the district took shape not as the result of some grandiose, far-sighted planning but rather in response to the needs of the day. **The Church of Our Lady before Týn** (Kostel P. Marie před Týnem) looms mightily from behind the Gothic buildings which close the square to the east. **The Týn School** and adjacent **House at the White Unicorn** (Dům U bílého jednorožce) almost seem to cower in her presence as they deny her access to the square below. It may seem odd that the largest and most beautiful church in the Old Town should not open directly onto the square that it so obviously dominates with her many turreted steeples, so distinctive a feature of the Prague skyline. This is due to the fact that the original church on this site, a much smaller structure dating from 1135, was built by the hospice of foreign merchants in the Týn Ungeld and was never intended to be a feature of the Old Town Square. By the late

Peter Parler's tympanum from the Church of Our Lady before Týn. National Gallery, Convent of St. George.

fourteenth century, when it started to be rebuilt in its present form on the previously consecrated site, the early Gothic cores of the buildings which front it today were already in place.
Construction work on the church started in 1365, during the reign c Charles IV. By the 1380s the choir along with the arches and walls of the main and lateral naves were completed. The north portal with its exquisitely carved tympanum depicting scenes from Christ's Passion (original now in the National Gallery's collection of Bohemian art situated next to the Basilica of St. George in Prague Castle) is the work of Peter Parler, Prague's foremost Gothic architect. During the Hussite wars (1419-34) this was the main town church where, from 1424, Jan Rokycana, later to become the first Hussite Archbishop, delivered his sermons to the attentive congregation. Under the elected Hussite King George of Poděbrady the church was finally finished with the construction of the west gable and the addition of the two steeples. Originally this was surmounted by a statue of the king with a drawn sword and a golde chalice, a symbol of the Utraquist doctrine. These, together with the words "The Truth Prevails," were summarily removed after the Battle of the White Mountain in 1620 — a grimly ironic portent for the prevailing conditions of more recent years.
Entrance to the church is gained through the Týn School in front of the west facade. Like so many other churches in Prague the original

Right
Golz-Kinský Palace.

The Church of Our Lady before Týn seen through the arcade at the top of the Old Town Hall Tower.

othic appearance of the interior has succumbed to the verwhelming influence of the Baroque. Damage caused by the Great ire of 1679 meant that the main vault had to be replaced although, ankfully, the Gothic vaulting of the lateral naves has been reserved intact. Behind a Gothic pulpit dating from the fifteenth entury stands the marble tombstone of the celebrated Danish tronomer Tycho de Brahe. Brahe came to Prague in 1597, where e took up the position of Court Astronomer to Emperor Rudolf II 1599. The observations he made while here in Prague were used y Johannes Kepler, another astronomer brought to the city at udolf's behest, as the basis for his laws on the movement of the anets. Kepler's laws, however, which related to the movement of e planets round the sun, were in contrast with geocentric view of e universe held by Brahe. The high altar bears a panel depicting e Ascension of our Lady and the Holiest Trinity by Karel Škréta 649), the leading exponent of Baroque painting whose works ecorate a large number of original and restyled Baroque churches. estling in between the Týn School and the Golz-Kinský Palace with s exuberant Rococo facade the **House at the Stone Bell** strikes a ote of cool, Gothic dignity. During the reign of John of Luxemburg 310-1348) the early Gothic building was transformed into this onumental tower and probably functioned as a town palace for Queen Elizabeth, daughter of Wenceslas II. The richly decorated

The Gothic House at the Stone Bell adds to the architectural diversity of the Old Town Square.

window linings and statuary niches on the exterior had been preserved for centuries beneath a Baroque facade which, following extensive architectural and archaeological research from 1973-87, was removed and the building restored to its former Gothic glory. The interior, with preserved fragments of delicate early Gothic frescoes, now houses temporary exhibitions from the National Gallery's collection of graphic art.

Returning to the square one should mention that its proportions look slightly different today to how they did before the 8th May 1945 when, during the Prague uprising, the Nazis razed the Neo-Gothic east wing of the Town Hall to the ground. Under the Communists

The Baroque Church of St. Nicholas dominates the northern corner of the Old Town Square.

ıere were supposed to have been plans to reconstruct the area now ıarked by a long patch of grass but to this day nothing has been one. This is perhaps no bad thing for the harmonious eclecticism of ıe square is enhanced by the presence of the finely proportioned aroque facade of the **Church of St. Nicholas** (1732-35), which was reviously consigned to relative ignominy in the narrow street of U adnice. The architect of this church was Killian Ignaz Dietzenhofer, ho went on to create the masterly Church of St. Nicholas in the Malá Strana.

On the north side of the square the sombre sculptural grouping of ıe **Jan Hus Monument** has surveyed the scene since it was set in

Looking up into the dome of St. Nicholas in the Old Town.

place in 1915 to commemorate the 500th anniversary of the martyrdom of the leader of the Hussite reform movement. In 1968 when the tanks of the Warsaw Pact rolled into the square to put an end to the liberalist tendencies that occasioned the Prague Spring, the monument was draped in black, mourning the loss of new-found liberties.

Any of the riddle of medieval streets that run south from the coronation route, as it continues into the Malé Náměstí down Jilská and right into Karlova, are worth exploring. Jilská, Michalská and Melantrichova are all interconnected by Gothic and Renaissance alleyways which run through the typically deep medieval building plots. In fact, if you have time to spare, it is almost worth throwing your map away and pitting your wits and nose for direction against

Ladislav Šaloun's monument to Jan Hus, set up in 1915 to commemorate the 500th anniversary of his martyrdom.

ne narrow and winding streets which almost constitute a living naze. Just past No. 18 Jilská, a passageway opens up on the left which leads through a palace courtyard with Renaissance arcades and nto the end of Michalská. Bear left and the alley opens into another ourtyard, this time containing the dilapidated Baroque **Church of St. Michael**. The former Gothic church which stood on this site was ome at various times throughout the fifteenth century to a uccession of Hussite preachers, including Jan Hus himself. The ervite monastery (1636-64), of which the church was a part, was bolished like so many others under Emperor Josef II, in an mbitious attempt to subjugate the Catholic Church to his rule. Once you emerge into Melantrichova, take a right and follow the treet a short distance till it is crossed by Havelská. The area

closed by this street and those that run parallel to it between the
elný trh (Coal Market) to the west and the Ovocný trh (Fruit
arket) to the east, housed the immense Gall market, known as the
w Market at its foundation to distinguish it from the one already
existence on the Old Town Square. Standing at the Uhelný trh
d and looking up towards the **Church of St. Gall (Kostel svatého
vla)** the original proportions of the square can still be discerned
spite the intrusion of subsequent building developments, which,
hough they bisected it, thankfully preserved the long runs of
thic arcading. Here, medieval merchants laid out their wares
tected from the intrusive inclemency of the weather. The Gothic
urch which stood on the site of the present Baroque structure of
. Gall was at the time one of the most important churches in the
ole of Prague and acted as the parish church for the Gall Town.
om 1363 to 1369 it was the scene for the reformist, puritanical
mons preached by Konrad Waldhauser, who had been invited to
ague with the approval of Charles IV by the first Archbishop,
nest of Pardubice.
hind the church, at the junction of Rytířská and Železná, stands
e Neo-Classical **Tyl Theatre** which was opened in 1783 as the
stitz Theatre. It was here on 29th October 1787 that the world
emiere of Mozart's *Don Giovanni* took place, written especially for
s Prague audience who, in contrast to the Viennese, had received
e Marriage of Figaro with rapturous enthusiasm. While in Prague,
ozart stayed with the Dušek family in their villa **Bertramka**,
uated in Mozartova in the Smíchov district of the city; the
ilding now houses the Mozart Museum.
ext to the Tyl Theatre, at Železná No.9, stands the **Carolinum**, the
re of the university founded by Charles IV in 1348, and the first
Central Europe. Although the hub of its activities is now located
re, at its foundation there was no permanent site, lectures taking
ace in churches and monasteries and even in the houses of the
asters themselves. It was not until 1383 that the university found a
rmanent home with the donation by Wenceslas IV of the Gothic
use of the Master of the Mint, Jan Rotlev. Like the Town Hall,
e original Gothic buildings of the Carolinum developed organically,
ditions to the complex being made by the purchase of surrounding
ildings, which were then adapted to serve their new function. The
autiful Gothic oriel window which protrudes from the Baroque
uthern facade is by the workshop of Peter Parler, also responsible
r the oriel of the chapel in the Old Town Hall.
e university was split into four administrative bodies catering for
e scholars of different nationalities who came to study here — the
zechs, the Poles, the Saxons and the Bavarians — and, in the
iversal spirit of the times, the four groups were also symbolic of
e four points of the compass. In 1398 Jan Hus was appointed to
e university as Professor of Philosophy. From this time on it
came the forum for hotly contested debates regarding the divisions
tween secular and religious power and the widespread, virulent
rruption within the Catholic Church.
the delicate balance between secular and religious authority,
clesiastical offices were more often than not awarded in the spirit

The spires of St. Gall.

St. Martin's is the oldest preserved rotunda in Prague.

of political expediency. It was a time of crisis within the Roman Catholic Church. The Holy See was transferred to Avignon to escap the bloody internal feuds rife in Rome at the time, giving rise to th great schism of dual papacy which was to last until 1415.
The seeds of reform had taken root following the closer contact wit England, engendered by the marriage of Anna, a daughter of Charl IV, to King Richard II in 1381. Czech students, returning from study periods at Oxford University, brought with them the books o John Wyclif which provided the philosophical basis for a return to religious piety in concordance with the original teachings of the Bible. These ideas were not well received by the other nations who were in a majority at the university nor, not surprisingly, by the clergy. The church, already weakened by the schism of dual papacy, was not keen to have its power undermined still further by the advance of popular reform. In any case, Hus was safe for the time being from reprisals by the Church, enjoying as he did the patronag of Wenceslas IV. The Archbishop of Prague supported the Roman Pope in opposition to Wenceslas, who favoured the Pope-elect in Pisa. The Archbishop, who needed the King's support to bring actic against Hus, was powerless while they continued to conflict over th point. Hus reinforced his position when he managed to persuade th King to alter the voting structure within the university, thanks to t decree of Kutná Hora in 1409 which gave the Bohemians three vot to the other nations' one. Four years later, however, Hus's position became extremely precarious, because he frustrated the King's plans by condemning the sacrilegious sale of indulgences, the proceeds of which were intended to help finance the war of the Pisan Pope against the Pope in Rome. Fearing possible repercussions, Hus left Prague and spent two years in the protection of his friends from th minor nobility. In his absence the reform party became more radica under the direction of Jakoubek of Stříbro, who declared the Pope Antichrist and instigated the serving of the the Holy Communion i both ways (*sub utraque specie* — which led to the reformers also being known as Utraquists).
Until then the lay people could only partake of the body of Christ Communion, the blood being reserved expressly for the clergy, as their privilege.
Hus came out of hiding in 1415 to defend his views at the Council of Constance, having accepted a guarantee of safe conduct from Emperor Sigismund. This, however, proved to be worthless. In Constance he was arrested and sentenced to be burnt at the stake f holding the Wyclifite heresies. After his martyrdom Hus was venerated as a saint, and the reform movement, which previously ha been known as Wyclifite, took on the name Hussite, although the reformers were also called Utraquist or Calixtines after their symbol a chalice.
The church where the first Utraquist communion took place, St. Martin in the Wall, is tucked away in Martinská, a street which ru out of Uhelný trh to the west. The original Romanesque church on this site, dating from 1178, the nave of which is preserved in the present church, served the needs of a village community that spread southwards in the direction of the present New Town.

Rotunda of the Holy Cross.

t that time the little Romanesque churches were not part of a ıified town complex but rather stood as the focus of small dividual village communities, the real process of urbanization being stricted to the area around the Old Town Square. Apart from the omanesque elements preserved in the basements of later Gothic ɔuses, architectural reminders of that prosperous period in the Old own are extremely scant. Around this time there were for example venty Romanesque rotundas of which only three have survived: one the New Town, **St. Longinus** in Na Rybníčku; one at Vyšehrad, **t. Martin's**; and one here in the Old Town, the **Rotunda of the loly Cross** (sv.Kříž) in Karoliny Světlé.

/hen the Romanesque settlements were surrounded by walls in 231, the builders where possible made use of the natural defensive ɔportunities afforded by the terrain. Consequently, the **Church of t. Martin in the Wall** was separated from the village and even cluded in the fortifications, resulting in the rather bizarre name by hich it has been known to the present day. The appearance of the ıurch today is a result of the late Gothic reconstruction carried out efore 1488, when two lateral naves were added to the building hich had already been enlarged by the addition of a square resbytery in about 1350. Set into the wall of this is a ɔmmemorative plaque to the famous Brokoff family of sculptors, ho left their mark not only on the avenue of statues on Charles ridge but also on the figural decoration of palace facades — a presentative feature of Prague Baroque.

arrying on past the church, Martinská leads into Na Perštýně which as part of the old route connecting the two castles of Vyšehrad and radčany. Take a right and you are heading back towards the ɔronation route. About 100 yards to the left, Bethlehem Square pens off Husova. You can't miss the twin gabled roof of the ethlehem Chapel, with its austere facade, a blunt rejection of the tricate sculptural ornamentation favoured in secular and established ıurch projects, recalling the fact that this was the centre of the form movement, the embryonic Hussites. Although this is a odern reconstruction from 1954, the original church of 1381 having ın to ruin, it is faithful to the plans of its historic predecessor. You ight ask why the Communist government of the day should spend oney on such a restoration project when they followed a largely heistic policy which resulted in the defrocking of many priests, ɔnsigning them to menial labour, and the expulsion of others. The ajority of smaller churches were closed and they now wait sadly for novation, like derelict amnesiacs hoping that their memories might ne day be restored to them. In fact the rebuilding of the chapel was ınctioned by the first Communist President and Prime Minister, lement Gottwald, on the grounds that in 1521 the German peasant gurehead, Thomas Münzer, had preached here, illustrating his rophetic vision of a communistic state: Gottwald felt that this made ideal as a monument to the long history of Communist ideals in rague.

ontinuing up Husova, we come to one of the few churches in the ld Town to have preserved its original Gothic exterior. The ɔnstruction of the **Church of St. Giles** (sv. Jilji) was begun by the

shop of Prague, Jan of Dražice, around 1310 and completed by the rchbishop, Ernest of Pardubice, in 1371. Jan of Dražice was an thusiastic propagator of the new Gothic style with which he had come acquainted during his long stay at the Papal Court in vignon. In Prague the Gothic had not been filtered through ermany but derived directly from France where it had originated; e earliest Gothic buildings in the city were built by Cistercian asons from Burgundy. As more and more people moved into the wn they were followed by various monastic orders, many of whom, the ongoing atmosphere of moral disintegration, lived in a ofligate manner, falling victim to the vices that accompanied the ore variegated urban lifestyle.

ne Convent of St. Agnes (a visit to which is best combined with a ur of Josefov) is a case in point: here nuns and monks lived in such ose proximity that it was only a matter of time before suspicions ere aroused. The convent was founded in 1233 by Wenceslas I at e instigation of his sister Agnes of Bohemia. Agnes introduced the rder of the Poor Clares, the female branch of the Franciscan order, to Bohemia and in 1235 she became abbess of the newly nstructed convent. The nuns originally had the use of the adjacent **hurch of St. Francis**, but around 1240 monks from the recently mpleted Minorite monastery took over the church whose windows parently looked through into the dormitory of the nuns! Thus nied their place of worship, the nuns set about building a new urch which was later enlarged by the addition of a presbytery and nsecrated to the Holy Saviour in the 1280s. Agnes herself was ried here along with other members of the Premsylid dynasty hose crowned heads form the sculptural decoration on the large pitals of the columns supporting the triumphal arch of the church. arious alterations were carried out during the fourteenth century, cluding the addition of an extra storey to the wings of the cloister d the construction of a steeple and chapel dedicated to St. Barbara the Church of St. Francis. This chapel was badly damaged in the re of 1689 after which it was given the Baroque restoration which s survived to the present day.

uring the Protestant Hussite uprising of 1420 the Catholic sisters ed for their lives, leaving the convent deserted for well over a ntury. From 1556 to 1626 it was occupied by the Dominicans, who d been ejected by the Jesuits from the monastery at St. Clement. he Poor Clares finally returned in 1627 when their fears had ssibly been allayed by the Imperial ordinance of that year which ade Catholicism the only permissible religion. In 1782 the convent as finally abolished and converted into a storehouse and dwelling ace for the poor. Today many of the convent buildings have been stored to their former Gothic glory and house part of the collection the National Gallery.

he number of monastic orders, invited from abroad, increased ring the reign of Charles IV, a policy designed to enhance the estige and reflect the international religious importance of the city, w that it had become the capital of the Holy Roman Empire. hese supplemented the Franciscans and Dominicans who had ready established themselves within the precincts of the Old Town

Left
The Church of St. Giles rises up above the bluff of the Old Town.

Carved pews in St. Giles.

— the Franciscans between the Convent of the Blessed Agnes (Agne was only canonized in 1990) and the **Church of St. James** (sv. Jakub and the Dominicans around the **Church of St. Clement** (sv. Kliment in Karlova. Incidentally, the acoustics in St. James are so remarkable that the organ in this church simply *has* to be heard.
The Dominicans were displaced when the Jesuits were summoned to Prague by the Habsburgs, in their remorseless battle to reinstitute Catholicism. Between 1556 and 1593 they systematically purchased land and property around the Church of St. Clement over an area o two hectares to make way not only for the Church of the Holy Saviour on Crusader Knights Square, but also for the massive expanse of the Jesuit College of the **Clementinum**.
In the area now encompassed by its walls there once stood about twenty-five houses as well as several churches and the monastery buildings attached to the original church of St. Clement, after which the complex was named. The expansionist doctrine of the Jesuits eventually led to their taking over of the Carolinum in 1656, when i was merged with the Clementinum to become the Charles-Ferdinand University. Although the exterior, articulated only by a rather monotonous ranging of Corinthian pilasters, is somewhat subdued (with the exception of the southern facade which is enlivened by the presence of the rotunda of the Italian Chapel between the Holy Saviour and St. Clement), in the interior three rooms in particular retain the magnificence of the high Baroque. The first, known as the **Baroque Hall**, houses the State Library of Czechoslovakia and is decorated with ceiling frescoes of the Muses and impressive *trompe l'oeil* compositions by J.Hiebl (1727), while the second, the **Mathematical Hall**, adorned with original Rococo stucco work, holds a permanent exhibition of eighteenth-century table clocks. Beneath the dome of the **Astronomical Tower** are displayed some of the mathematical and astronomical instruments used in the experiments of Tycho de Brahe.
There are times in Prague when, despite the grandeur of the Baroque, one cannot but help being reminded of the wholesale destruction that took place to accommodate the redevelopment. But there are also times when the Baroque, applied sensitively, achieved rare harmony with earlier existing structures. One example of this is the recently restored **House at The Golden Well** (Dům U zlaté studně) on the corner of Seminářská and Karlova, where the application of Baroque stucco reliefs of popular saints enhances the simple lines of the Renaissance structure.
You will have noticed by now that the majority of houses are referred to by their romantic, folklorish signs. As in so many fields, the romantic sufferred at the hands of the rational, when in the mid eighteenth century Empress Maria Theresa urged the allocation of house numbers to replace the beautiful but outmoded mediaeval system. But although the postal system is governed numerically, numbers and pictures co-exist peacefully on the exteriors of many buildings. Golden is an epithet that abounds — At the Golden Tree (U zlatého stromu), At the Golden Tiger (U zlatého tygra), At the Golden Scales (U zlaté váhy) — its use originating in Rudolfinian literature, where Caroline Prague became the "Golden City." This

ferred in particular to the gilding of the roofs of the castle gates
arried out by Charles IV so that they might act as beacons, visible
om great distances, declaring the fame and prosperity of the city.
hereafter its popularity spread like a benevolent virus so that now it
ems there is not a street left untouched by the hand of Midas and
night, on Charles Bridge, even the silence bears his fingerprints.
n the corner of Liliová and Karlova stands the Renaissance house
t the Golden Serpent (U zlatého hada) which was home in 1714 to
e owner of the first coffee house in Prague, the Armenian
eodatus Damajan. This was located in the **House at the Three**
striches (U tří pštrosů) next to Charles Bridge in the Malá Strana
nd would have provided valuable sustenance in the winter for those
aving the bitter winds that course up the Vltava, peeling the
rface of the river and turning the air-borne droplets to ice. The
ouse, with its fine Renaissance murals and painted ceilings, now
ouses a restaurant and hotel. Karlova finishes its journey by skirting
e walls of the Holy Saviour, the second church located within the
ecinct of the Clementinum, and opens out into the tiny square of
e Crusader Knights (Křižovnické náměstí). Today, however, the
ea feels less like a square than an extraordinarily picturesque
ossroads, where the stream of vehicles using the somewhat intrusive
mbankment road battles constantly with the pedestrian traffic
rging ever onwards towards the Charles Bridge.
he area of the bridgehead on the Old Town side was settled in
252 by the Czech order of the Knights of the Cross with a Red
tar, who had previously been attached to the hospice associated
ith the Convent of the Blessed Agnes. Here they built a hospital in
e crypt of the domed Baroque **Church of St. Francis**. This church,
uilt by J.B Mathey between 1679 and 1689, exists almost as the
int echo of St. Nicholas in Malá Strana, whose larger dome sings
ut from the other side of the Vltava, beckoning the traveller across
e wide waters like a benevolent Siren. Passing the statue of Charles
V, set up in 1848 to commemorate the 500th anniversary of the
unding of Charles University, we enter the long afternoon shadow
f the Old Town Bridge Tower. Begun in 1391, this magnificent
efensive gateway guarding what was then the only crossing of the
ltava, was the work of Peter Parler and his cathedral workshop.
lthough the western, bridge facade was badly damaged by Swedish
helling in 1648, the east still bears witness to the exceptional quality
f Bohemian Gothic sculpture. In the middle of the wall above the
ateway, ranged with the heraldic shields of those lands that were at
he time part of the Czech domains, are displayed a triumvirate of
articular significance to the bridge.
tanding in the centre, atop a relief representation of two bridge
rches, is the patron saint of the bridge, St. Vitus. On his right sits
harles IV wearing the Imperial crown while his son Wenceslas IV,
esponsible for the completion of the bridge, is enthroned to his left
earing the crown of a Roman King. The decorations once bore a
risly addition, however, when after the execution of the twenty-
even leaders of the anti-Habsburg rebellion, twelve of the rebels'
eads were fixed to the Tower and remained there for ten years,
rom 1621 to 1631.

harles Bridge, with its 520 meters of cobbled, pedestrian walkway, retches like a stone carpet between the Old Town and the Malá trana, the waters of the river splitting round each of its sixteen iers as if they were the petrified thighs of some stubborn and solute ogre. The first bridge on this site was built in 1118, a little the north of the present structure. This early wooden bridge was rn to pieces by flood waters in 1157 and replaced a year later by a ew stone bridge, the second oldest in Europe after Regensburg, nown eponymously as the Judith Bridge after King Vladislav II's cond wife. The smaller of today's two Malá Strana bridge towers is fact the original gateway to the earlier bridge, in whose interior is reserved one of the most important pieces of Prague Romanesque lief sculpture showing the King on his throne with what is probably figure representing the builder of the bridge kneeling by his side. he Judith Bridge sustained the insistent onslaught of the Vltava for early two hundred years before it too was destroyed by flooding in 342. The triumphant successor, started in 1357 by Peter Parler and mpleted in the early fifteenth century, has survived right down to e present day. Tradition has it that the mortar used in the nstruction had its binding power enhanced by the addition of eggs the mix. Charles IV himself was rumoured to have appealed to his eople to bring as many eggs as possible to the site, the story relating ow the peasants from the countryside responded by arriving with artloads — all of them unfortunately hardboiled! Whatever the ecret of its longevity, the bridge remains one of the most majestic nywhere, affording a promenade guarded by ranks of statuary that re themselves subject to the permanent vigil of an almost endless piral of gulls. This notion of an avenue of statues, borrowed from he Ponte Sant'Angelo in Rome, harnessed the skills of some of the est Baroque sculptors in Prague to steal these silent attendants from he roll of popular Czech hagiography. The oldest piece of sculpture n the bridge is the bronze crucifix by J. Hilger (1629), set in its lace (third on the right from the Old Town Bridge Tower) in 1657. he incongruity of the Hebrew lettering set round the cross results rom an incident in 1695, when a member of the Jewish community as ordered by the courts to install it by way of atoning for his buse of Christ, who was naturally unable to sue for slander on his wn behalf. This statue, together with that of St. John of Nepomuk ighth on the right from the Old Town Bridge Tower) are the only wo to be made of bronze. All the others, with the exception of that f St. Philip Benizi (third on the left from the Malá Strana bridge owers) which is marble, are fashioned from sandstone. Due to the oftness of this stone a number of the originals have now been emoved to the lapidarium of the State Museum, their place having een taken by copies. The figure of John of Nepomuk is a relatively ecent addition to Catholic hagiography, having been canonized in 729 as a symbol of revitalized Catholicism. But the reason for his anonization was based on an erroneous account of his martyrdom at he hands of Wenceslas IV in 1393. This relates how John of Pomuk, he Archbishop of Prague at the time, was tortured and thrown into he Vltava for not revealing the details of the Queen's confession to er husband.

Prague's first coffee house, the House at the Three Ostriches.

Charles Bridge. The Old Town Bridge Tower guards the entrance to the Old Town.

Following pages
Charles Bridge. The particular atmosphere of the avenue of Saints.

Charles Bridge. M. B. Mandl: Statue of St. Philip Benizi (1714).

J. Hilger's bronze Crucifix (1629).

Henceforth he was known as Nepomuk (ne means no in Czech) for his refusal to submit to the will of the monarch, thereby commending himself for subsequent canonization as a staunch upholder of confessional rights. In fact he was martyred because he defended the rights of the church against the encroachment of secular power. Whether or not the adherence to the apocryphal version was a deliberate avoidance of the truth is not clear; however it did conveniently sidestep any reference to an issue which, in the early eighteenth century, was becoming topical once more, namely the balance of temporal power between the state and the church.

M. B. Braun: wooden statue of St. Jude Taddens (1712). National Gallery, Convent of St. George.

View down the Vltava from Letná Hill.

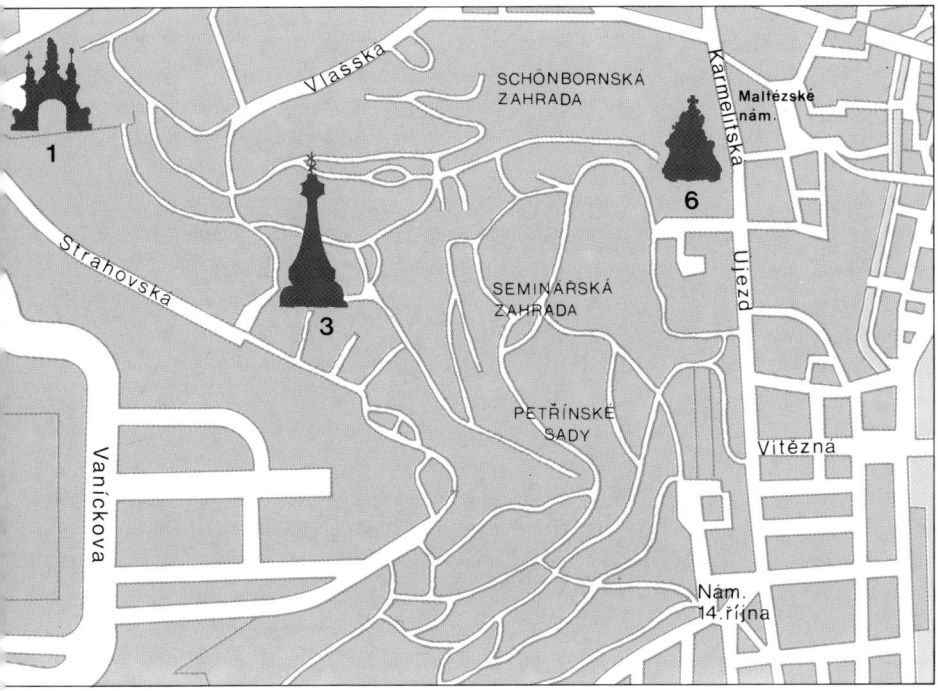

MALÁ STRANA

The area on the west bank of the Vltava, clinging to the banks between the Letná and Petřín hills and climbing the slopes of the Hradčany spur, is known as Malá Strana or Lesser Quarter. Like much of the Old Town, it is dominated by the Baroque although beneath that vestigial decoration the cores of many buildings are much older. This was the second town of Prague, founded in 1257 by Přemysl Otakar II (1253-1278) with the aim of unifying the scattered Romanesque settlements that had grown up in the castle's shadow. However, this move was not meant to provide for his own people, whom he moved out to a village nearby, instituting colonists from Northern Germany in their place and thereby sowing the seeds of nationalist friction which were to sprout and take root at various periods in the future. In order to make the opportunity more enticing they were offered assorted tax incentives and granted the right to be governed by Magdeburg law.

At its foundation it was called the New Town (Nové Město) to distinguish it from its slightly earlier counterpart across the river and only became known as the Lesser Quarter with the establishment of Charles IV's New Town in 1348. In its early days the area was not really on an equal footing with the Old Town as it depended almost entirely on the castle for its livelihood. Added to this, its administrative powers were severely limited by the domination of the territory by the two monastic orders of St. John and St. Thomas and by the encroachment of the Old Town citizens who were laying claim not only to the whole length of Charles Bridge but also to the banks of Malá Strana and even the lower slopes of Petřín Hill.

During the building boom under Charles IV the boundaries of the

Left
The dome of St. Nicholas marks Malá Strana from afar.

uarter were extended considerably and outlying settlements which ad previously been excluded from the protection of the Premyslid ortifications were encompassed by the new walls built around 1360. 'he section of this wall that runs up the southern end of the Petřín Iill is known as the **Hunger Wall** as it supposedly provided work for he town's builders at a time when starvation threatened, after a rolonged period of unemployment.

The Hunger Wall glimpsed through the trees that surround the Church of St. Lawrence on Petřín Hill.

Jone of these fortifications, however, were able to protect the istrict from the destruction wrought by the rebellious Hussite itizens in the first quarter of the fifteenth century, when much of he area was laid waste in the course of their battles against the royal arrison stationed at Prague Castle.

t was to be the best part of fifty years before Malá Strana recovered rchitecturally from the devastation and even then the fabric of the own lasted only until 1541, when a merciless fire ravaged the whole uarter, its flames penetrating the castle complex and damaging the s yet incomplete St. Vitus Cathedral. Although it is unfortunate that o much of the original Gothic buildings were claimed by the onflagration, in a way it was a propitious event for the rooting of Renaissance architecture in Prague, providing as it did the pportunity for a widescale remodelling of the quarter.

'hat it occurred a mere fifteen years after the accession of the ighty Austrian Habsburgs to the throne of Bohemia meant that oth the political motivation and the economic conditions were ideal or the restructuring of Malá Strana. Whole families of Italian raftsmen were imported to assist in the operation, many of them ettling in and around the street Vlašská. Although the character of Malá Strana was largely modelled during the Baroque period, much f the underlying framework is the result of this Renaissance econstruction.

'he atmosphere one encounters on crossing into Malá Strana is quite istinct from that of the Old Town on the other side of the river. Jespite the fact that it was founded as a commercial centre, perating from what still is the central focus — the **Lesser Quarter quare** (Malostranské náměstí) — Malá Strana really came into its wn after the Battle of the White Mountain in 1620 when wealthy amilies loyal to the victorious Habsburgs settled in the area. Here hey found large tracts of land abandoned by the members of the Bohemian nobility and burghers who had refused to adopt the Catholic faith and who had therefore been forced to emigrate.

'he widespread availability of land and its proximity to the Castle, vith whose scale and grandeur many of the remaining nobles sought o compete, provided the ideal circumstances for them to indulge in mbitious building projects and the laying out of magnificent summer ardens which, together with the green expanses of the Petřín and etná Hills, imbue the surroundings with the quality of an ristocratic playground.

'he proportions of the present square remain much as they were at he foundation of the Gothic town, although, as in the case of the Old Town Square, the Gothic cores of the buildings are hidden ehind Renaissance and Baroque facades dating from subsequent edevelopments. The space is dominated by the massive presence of

Mostecká - on the coronation route to the Castle.

Right
The Church of St. Nicholas dwarfs the other buildings in the square.

the high Baroque **Church of St. Nicholas** (Chrám svatého Mikuláše) and the adjoining former Jesuit college. Together they divide the square into two, as indeed it had been from the outset when the central portion was occupied by the Gothic Church of St. Nicholas (founded in 1283), its attendant rectory and graveyard and a Romanesque rotunda of St. Wenceslas. In 1625, shortly after the Battle of the White Mountain, the Gothic church was donated to the Jesuits; over the following decades they built their college, the first of several in Prague, established to train the large number of clerics necessary for the reinstitution of Catholicism. It was not until 1704, however, that work was started on a church whose magnitude was in keeping with the scale of the mission of conversion on which the order had embarked. This new church was initiated by Christian Dientzenhofer, who built the basilica which forms the nave of the

MALOSTRANSKÁ

church today. It was his son, however, Kilian Ignaz, who went on to extend the church by adding a sacristy surmounted by the great dome which, together with Lurago's finely proportioned belfry tower has become the symbol not only of Malá Strana but also of the triumph of Catholicism and of its visual vehicle, the Baroque. The interior is no less impressive, with its vast ceiling fresco in the nave (1500 sq. metres) ranking as one of the largest paintings in Europe. It is the sheer scale of the details, such as the gargantuan statues of church teachers that guard the piers of the dome, which generates an atmosphere of restrained power, unlike some other Baroque interiors where the force is lost beneath a clutter of overweight decoration that excludes the light and roots the imagination to the floor, when it should be sent soaring vaultward. The first Baroque church to be built in Prague is situated in Malá Strana on Karmelitská. Ironically, bearing in mind that Baroque was the style of the Counter-Reformation, the church was built and consecrated to the Holy Trinity by the community of German Lutherans on the site of a former Hussite church. After the Battle of the White Mountain it was donated by the Emperor to the order of the bare-footed Carmelites, who rebuilt it and reconsecrated it to **St. Mary Victorious** (Kostel P. Marie Vítězné), thereby hinting at the bellicose strain of the Counter-Reformation and its positive missionary zeal. Inside is a rather unusual object of spiritual contemplation, a wax doll brought from Spain and donated to the church by Polyxena of Lobcowicz in 1628. This celebrated miniature mannequin, much like the one in the Church of Aracoeli in Rome, is dressed by nuns in ornately embroidered robes and precious jewels, votive gifts from noble Catholic ladies. He looks down from his extravagantly embellished display case on pilgrims from all over the world, who flock here to address their prayers to the doll in the hope that faith in his ability as a miracle worker is well founded. In the catacombs beneath the church, the bodies of Carmelite friars in a miraculous state of preservation would probably testify that it is. At the lower north east corner of the square stands the late Renaissance **Lesser Town Hall** (Malostranská radnice) which administered the cultural, political and economic affairs of Malá Strana until 1784, when the towns of Prague were unified and run as a single unit. Before this the heterogeneous character of the towns was mirrored by a corresponding diversity of religious belief which, since the beginning of the Hussite Wars, had split the population into clearly definable factions. These included offshoots of the original Utraquist reform movement, further diversified by their adhesion to the northern European Calvinist or Lutheran trends. Towards the end of the sixteenth century the division between the Catholic, monarchical autocracy of the Habsburgs and the Protestant Bohemian Estates had deepened, but the Estates still had considerable bargaining power at the Czech Diet, or Land Registry. When in 1575 Maximilian II sought the approval of the Estates to raise an extra levy for a campaign against the Turks in Hungary, along with acceptance of his son Rudolf as the future King, the Estates agreed on condition that he in return should grant tolerance to non-Catholics. Realizing that Ferdinand would try and exploit the internal division of the different arms of Protestantism, they strengthened the tenor of their

The Church of St. Mary Victorious.

The Church of St. Nicholas with Dientzenhofer's dome and Lurago's belfry. A synthesis of German and Italian influences results in the definitive Prague Baroque church.

emand by grouping under a common front and signing a concordat nown as the Bohemian Confession, the terms of which were hrashed out here in the Lesser Town Hall. Although Maximilian's oncessions were not as far reaching as might have been hoped and othing was committed to writing for posterity, he did accept the xistence of a Protestant establishment.

t was not until 1609, however, that the Protestant demands for eligious freedom were granted by Rudolf II in his charter known as he Letter of Majesty, and then only because he required their upport to counter the ambitions of his younger brother Matthias, vho himself had designs on the Bohemian throne. The mood of olerance and religious pluralism did not last long, however, and the erennial differences surfaced once more when, prompted by a clear iolation of the terms of the charter by certain members of the overnment, the Estates convened and plotted the downfall of the rrant ministers. This meeting took place in the late Renaissance **miřický Palace** (No. 18/6), which dominates the north-western orner of the square, on May 22nd 1618. And from this palace the ext day a group of representatives departed for the castle to carry

The Waldstein garden.

out what became known as the Second Defenestration of Prague. Although no one was seriously injured, due to the fortuitous positioning of a pile of excrement and general refuse below the window from which they were thrown, this action lit the fuse for the Battle of the White Mountain, which in turn ignited the pan-European conflict of the Thirty Years War.

The whole northern end of the upper square is closed by the **Lichtenstein Palace** which takes its name from the notorious governo Karel of Lichtenstein. Known as the Bloody Governor for his remorseless persecution of the leaders of the anti-Habsburg uprising, he was ultimately responsible for the mass executions on the Old Town Square and the subsequent display of the heads on the Old Town Bridge Tower.

Leaving the square via Tomášská takes you in the direction of what is without doubt the grandest and most opulent of the Baroque palaces in Malá Strana — the Waldstein. As in the Old Town it is advisable to look up from time to time so as not to miss details on the facades of buildings that might otherwise go unnoticed. Set above an entrance (No. 4/26) about half way along Tomášská on the right, for example, is perhaps the most sculpturally ornate of Prague' house signs depicting St. Hubert and a stag, by F.M. Brokoff.

hortly afterward the street opens up into Waldstein Square
/aldštejnské náměstí), the whole east side of which is taken up by
ıe facade of the early Baroque palace of the same name. At first
ght **Waldstein Palace**, despite its evident size, does not look like a
uilding that could compete in scale and grandeur with the Castle
omplex on Hradčany; but one only has to follow its perimeter wall
l the way along Valdštejnská, taking a right into Klárov and trace
ıe return wall running up Letenská, to realize that the facade by
omparison is but a humble apology for the embarrassment of riches.
he man behind this imposing group of buildings, which is almost
ke a self-contained town, was the phenomenally successful and
onsequently enormously wealthy general, Albrecht of Wallenstein
583-1634). Wallenstein had made his name and personal fortune as
condottiere in the service of Ferdinand II, rising to become the
nperial Generalissimo during the Thirty Years War. Having been
warded the title of Duke of Friedland, he profited greatly from the
onfiscation of property belonging to the Czech nobility in the wake
f the Battle of the White Mountain, amassing the finances necessary
o embark on his ambitious project in Malá Strana. His was to be
ıe first of the mighty Baroque palaces that proliferate in the
uarter, a palace which was composed of five interconnecting
ourtyards and a magnificent garden held in the embrace of rambling
ings that spread almost to the foot of Letná Hill. Twenty-five
ouses and three private gardens were bought up and demolished to
ake way for the dynastic home which was to stay in the family
ght up until 1945. Although the interior now houses the Ministry
f Education and is therefore inaccessible, the splendid Italianate
arden is open during the spring and summer (entrance in Letenská).
esigned and built exclusively by Italians, the Latin influence is
owhere more apparent than in the combination of statuary, artificial
ools and grottoes ranged around the central axis deriving from the
chly frescoed, triple-arched loggia. This was said to be the source of
/allenstein's greatest pride and understandably so, casting as it does
s triocular gaze down the avenue of copies of bronze statues by
drien de Vries, court sculptor to Emperor Rudolf II. The originals,
ke many of the art treasures that existed on this side of the river,
ere looted by the Swedes during the Thirty Years War and now
eside in the grounds of Drottingholm Palace near Stockholm.
he vast scale of Wallenstein's palace, which is best appreciated from
ıe vantage point outside the lower east gate of the Castle, cocks an
most contemptuous snook at the residence of his Lord and Master
igh up on the Hradčany spur. Wallenstein, however, was a double
ealer whose ambitions ultimately o'erleapt themselves. Not satisfied
ith the pre-eminent position he had won for himself in the Imperial
ourt, he entered into clandestine negotiations with the opposing
orces of the Protestant cause who were offering him the Bohemian
rown in return for his support. Ferdinand II took no chances with
/allenstein's wavering allegiance, possibly recalling that he was in
ny case a convert to the Catholic fold, and had him murdered at
heb (at that day Eger) in western Bohemia. Waldstein Palace was
ıe first of many aristocratic residences that sprang up in Malá
trana, the stronghold of the predominantly German-speaking

Adrian De Vries: Hercules and the Golden Apples of the Hesperides. National Gallery, Convent of St. George.

Right
Waldstein Palace stucco and fresco work on the ceiling of the Sala Terrena.

nobility. Many of the streets and nearly all of the squares are littered with the palaces of powerful families such as the Lobcowicz, Kolowrat and Černín clans. On Valdštejnská alone there are four, perhaps most remarkable for their terraced gardens laid out on the slopes in the very shadow of the Castle. All of these, with the exception of the Fürstenberg garden which is the property of the Polish Embassy, are open to the public, access being gained by the entrance next to Kolowrat Palace (No.10/154).

The palaces no longer function as private residences, but thankfully they have been kept in use either as the offices of various Czech ministries or as the seats of foreign embassies. In fact Malá Strana is Prague's Embassy Land, the vast majority of them located in palaces in the streets Vlašská and Nerudova and in the tranquil Maltese (Maltézské) and Grand Priory (Velkopřevorské) squares. When there are no people around in these two pockets of untouched Baroque serenity it requires little imagination to transport oneself back to the days of frock coats and powdered wigs, of balls that Casanova himself attended, of gauntlets thrown down to the intricate lilt of chamber music and of scores settled at dawn while the mists from the Vltava still clung between the cobbles. Tycho de Brahe, Rudolf's astronomer, sacrificed his nose in one such duel, thereafter sporting a silver proboscis to hide his loss of face. **Maltese Square** takes its name from the Monastery of the Order of St. John, or Maltese Knights, who settled and fortified the bridgehead of the old Judith Bridge in 1169. The **Church of Our Lady Below the Chain** (Kostel Panny Marie pod řetězem) in Lázěnská formed the heart of the monastic buildings. Although the original Romanesque building was subject to an extensive Gothic reconstruction in the mid-fourteenth century, elements of the earlier structure are preserved in the courtyard of the present church behind the large prismatic towers which front the street. On the corner on the left where Lázěnská enters Grand Priory Square, is the Baroque palace of the same name (No.4/485) which now serves as the Museum of Czech Music and houses a fascinating collection of old musical instruments along with the musical archives of the National Museum. Further down the square, which is closed on the southern side by the French Embassy in the **Buquoy Palace**, there is a monument to a more recent brand of musical hero. On a stretch of wall, which under the Communists saw the frequent posting of guards to counter anti-establishment graffiti, Prague has its own John Lennon memorial next to images drawn from The Beatles along with slogans committed to the idea of freedom of speech. At the far end of the square a little bridge spans the branch of the river known as Čertovka and leads onto **Kampa Island**. Čertovka, which translates as The Devil's Stream, probably takes its name from an eccentric woman who lived in the house At the Seven Devils (U sedmi čertů) in Maltese Square. The island provides ideal respite from the crowds thronging over Charles Bridge and up to the Castle, as well as offering an unforgettable panorama of the bridge and the embankments of the Old Town running down towards the National Theatre with its roof crowned with gilded railings and glinting in the sun. In earlier days the blaze of colourful pageant that accompanied the coronation procession could be seen

PALLANTES
ENEAS

passing over Charles Bridge, up Mostecká, through the Lesser Town Square and, with horses breaking into a sweat, into the long climb o Nerudova. Yet more of the characteristic house signs proliferate along Nerudova as well as the straining, Baroque stone figures that support the portals and windows of palaces, such as the blackamoors set into the facade of **Morzin Palace**, or the eagles guarding the entrance to the Italian Embassy. At the top of Nerudova you can either follow the road round into Ke Hradu which brings you out in front of the castle, or take the steps (Zámecké schody) up into the western end of Hradčany Square.

"Prague Venice."

Right
House signs in Malá Strana.

HK

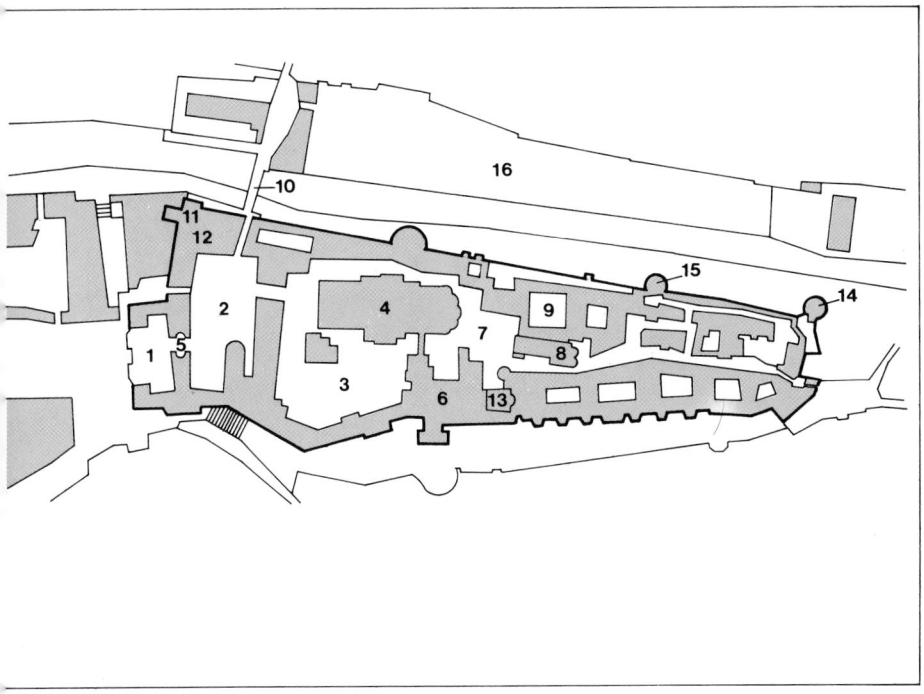

1. *First Courtyard*
2. *Second Courtyard*
3. *Third Courtyard*
4. *St. Vitus Cathedral*
5. *Matthias Gateway*
6. *Royal Palace*
7. *St. George Square*
8. *Basilica of St. George*
9. *Convent of St. George*
10. *Powder Bridge*
11. *Spanish Hall*
12. *Gallery*
13. *All Saints' Church*
14. *Dalibor's Tower*
15. *White Tower*
16. *Gardens*

HRADČANY CASTLE

'he castle spreads its massive wings like a huge bird of prey hovering bove Malá Strana on the west bank of the Vltava at the old fording oint of the ancient east-west trade route. Legend has it that the ıythical Princess Libuše, renowned for her prophetic powers, oresaw the great destiny in store for Prague. Perched high atop her esidence at Holy Vyšehrad she surveyed the forested slopes of the pposite bank, declaring in an oracular voice, "I can see a vast city hose fame reaches to the stars." Then she sent her followers into he forest with instructions to found a town at the point where they aw a ploughman called Přemysl building the threshold (prah) of a ouse. Hence the title of the dynasty — the Premyslids — and the ame of the city — Praha. According to some chroniclers these ıythical origins date from the eighth century. But archaeological vidence dates the construction of the first castle at the second half f the ninth century, when Duke Bořivoj, having conquered the Czech tribes who had settled below the escarpment, resolved to ortify it.

Attempting the summit of Hradčany via the precipitous streets of Nerudova and Vlašská, it is immediately apparent just why the Castle s so well sited. Initially, however, the Castle was no more than a vooden hilltop fort with earthen ramparts. It was not until the leventh century, during the reign of Břetislav I, that these were eplaced with a stone curtain wall two metres thick and further ortified with two towers at the east and west ends. One hundred ears later much of the present layout of the Castle complex was etermined by the building programme of Soběslav I (1125-1140), lthough he himself continued to reside upriver at Vyšehrad (High Castle).

n 1303 the Castle was gutted by fire and left deserted until 1333, hen Charles IV ordered its reconstruction during the reign of his

Prague Castle - part of the unmistakable skyline.

"I can see a vast city whose fame reaches to the stars."

Battling giants atop the gates to the First Courtyard.

The Castle gates.

father John of Luxemburg. Under Charles Prague was to become, with the extension of Malá Strana and the foundation of the New Town, the largest and most important city in Central Europe. Charles was one of the first of the highly erudite mediaeval European rulers. Educated in Paris by the later to be Pope Clement VII and married to a French princess, his contact with the cultural hub of Western Europe and his favourable relations with the Holy See, which was then in Avignon and dominated by the French, had far reaching effects on the growth of the city, both politically and artistically. His reconstruction of the Castle modelled itself after the designs of the great Gothic palaces in Paris, providing him not only with an elegant residence but also a potent symbol of Prague's elevated status in international affairs. Part of these palace buildings are preserved beneath the Vladislav Hall but, like much of the previous and subsequent structural developments, they were enshrouded by the large-scale but rather uninspiring Neo-Classical reconstruction commissioned during the eighteenth century by Empress Maria Theresa.

The present Castle is laid out around three interconnecting courtyards, the first of which opens onto Hradčany Square. This courtyard with its wrought iron, Rococo gates was built on top of th castle moat during the eighteenth-century redevelopment and provides the scene every day at midday for the changing of the palace guard. This used to be a solemn, grey, goose-stepping affair but now, aided by the splash of colour provided by the new uniform commissioned from Theodor Pištěk (the Oscar winning costume esigner for *Amadeus*, which was shot here in Prague), the young onscripts seem in an embarrassed sort of way to enjoy it as much as ne crowds of onlookers. From the tops of the gate piers copies of atues by I. F. Platzer (1768), muscle bound, battling giants look own in a swirl of motionless stone on the stock still guards who are etrified by comparison.

rossing the first courtyard we come to the stolid **Matthias Gate**, its ough hewn face imprisoned by the pale skinned embrace of the ings of Maria Theresa's palace. This gateway, built by Emperor Iatthias in 1614, was the first secular Baroque structure, providing a ee standing western entrance to the Castle before it was ncorporated in the eighteenth-century redevelopment. The austerity f the second courtyard acts as a sort of airlock before entering the rified atmosphere of the ancient core of the Castle grouped in and ound the third. A northern entrance which opens to our left fords access, via the **Powder Bridge** (Prašný Most) spanning the eer Pit, to the late Renaissance buildings of the **Riding School** and **ion's Den** at one end of the **Summer Garden** (open only in spring). aid out in 1534, this was one of the first gardens in the Italian yle north of the Alps. Although the design of the garden has nanged since then, its original ambience is maintained by the uildings of the **Ball Games Court** (Míčovna), built in Palladian style the court architect Bonifaz Wolmut and Ulrico Aostalis in 1567-9, and the magnificent **Summer Palace of Queen Anne**. This uilding, arguably the most beautiful Renaissance building north of ne Alps, with its unusual but elegant roof truss, like the upturned

Prague Castle: guards in new uniforms.

The Summer Palace of Queen Anne. The Italian architectural Renaissance arrives in Prague.

The remarkable "Singing Fountain."

"Singing Fountain," detail.

hull of a ship, was built between 1538 and 1563 at the behest of Emperor Ferdinand I (1526-1564), the first Habsburg to accede to the Bohemian throne. In effect this was the first building in Prague to be conceived from the outset in the spirit of the Italian Renaissance, giving impetus after the catastrophic fire of 1541 to other Bohemian noblemen for the construction of the Renaissance palaces which line Hradčany Square. Emperor Rudolf II (1576-1611) preferred to hold court here in the Summer Palace, listening to the haphazard voice of water on bronze produced by the **Singing Fountain** outside and maintaining the real world of politics and government at arm's length in the palace buildings on the other side of the Deer Pit. Rudolf it was that transformed the Castle of his da into a private museum to rival any in Europe, extending the castle along the northern wall of the second courtyard to house his remarkable collection, including works by Titian, Tintoretto, Veronese and Rubens as well as representative examples of Bohemia Baroque. But those that remain now, after the Swedish looting

Stromovka Park - Summer Pavilion.

uring the Thirty Years War and the German looting during the Nazi ccupation, are a pale shadow of the wonders with which Rudolf ırrounded himself in his lifetime. Then the collection was bolstered y the presence of masterpieces of both the southern and northern enaissance including paintings by Michelangelo, Leonardo Da Vinci, aphael, Giorgione, Dürer, Holbein, Cranach and Brueghel. Some of nese are preserved in the National Gallery's collection in the ternberg Palace, but all together they represent only a fraction of udolf's patronage and compulsive desire to collect. In 1619 an nventory revealed that the collection ran to some three thousand aintings and two and a half thousand sculptures and was valued at ne staggering sum of seventeen million guilders. Neither was this ompulsion limited to the field of the figurative arts, taking in as it id clocks, scientific apparatus and a bizarre range of relics and atural curiosities including what purported to be the nails from Noah's Ark and a phial of the dust from which God created Adam. 'he name of Rudolf is synonymous with the flowering of the

The east end of St. Vitus with its fan of ambulatory chapels.

Renaissance in Prague, at a time when many wealthy rulers were turning away from the problems agitating in the social structure in favour of pursuits that examined the outer rather than the inner world. Rudolf was a solitary, mentally unstable depressive who preferred to devote his attentions to the host of alchemists he had brought to the city in his quest for the Philosopher's Stone (including the English magician Edgar Kelley), or to the astronomers scouring the heavens for clues to the order of the universe. In this he bore a remarkable similarity to another phenomenally wealthy late Renaissance patron in the same period in Florence, Francesco de' Medici, perhaps revealing the confusion that the prolonged questioning of the Renaissance had wrought in the minds of those closest to its heart.

The area now taken up by the Third Courtyard was the centre of the first settlement on the Hradčany spur. Much of the remnants from the earlier building developments have been consumed by Picassi's eighteenth-century redevelopment for Empress Maria Theresa which now contain State Rooms and presidential offices. The western and southern wings, for example, have as their core the original Romanesque fortifications erected by Soběslav I in the second quarter of the twelfth century and the lowest floor of the Old Royal Palace still contains the mighty barrel vaulting of the Soběslav Hall. The square is dominated, however, by the soaring presence of **St. Vitus Cathedral**, which commands the skyline for miles lifted aloft by

Left
St. Vitus from Nový Svět.

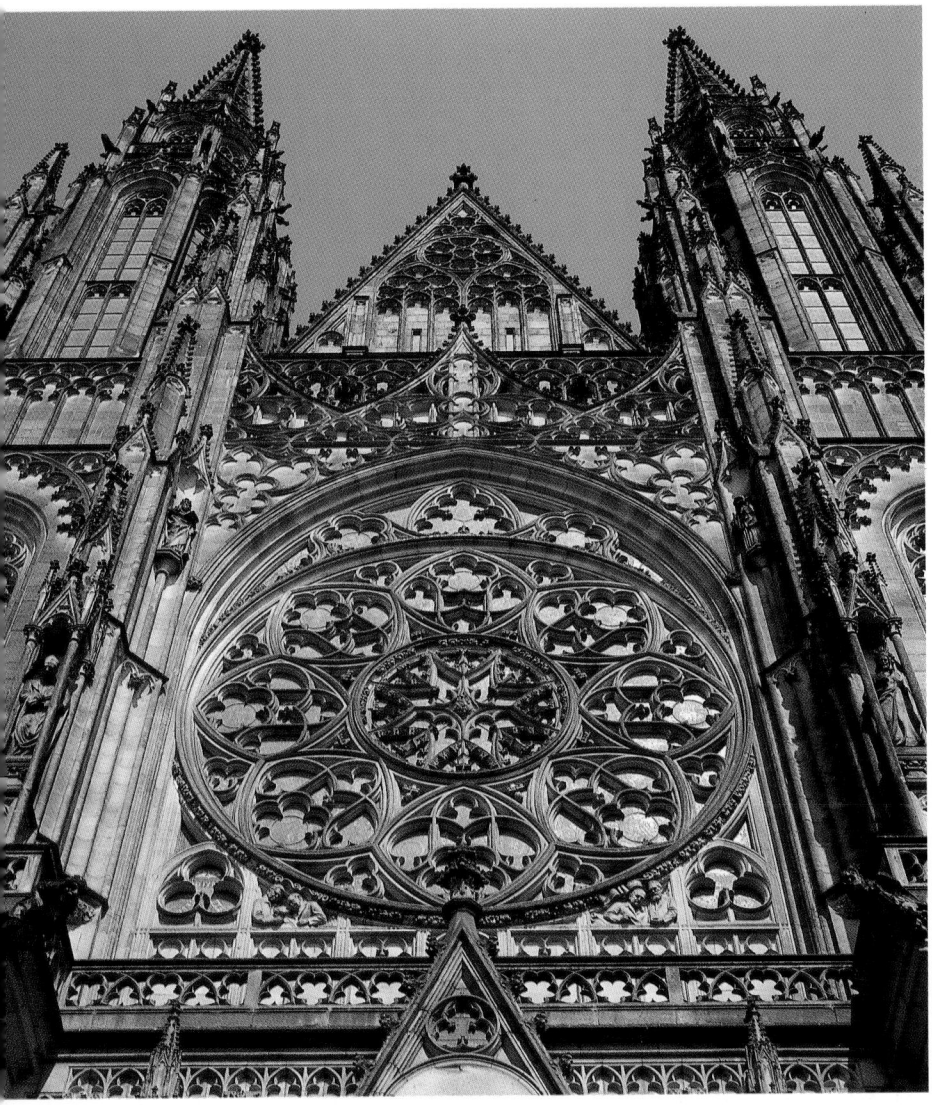

St. Vitus: the South Tower and Golden Gate.

St. Vitus: the Rose Window.

ıe powerful shoulders of the precipitous rocky outcrop of the Iradčany. The first church on this particular site, the Romanesque **Rotunda of St. Vitus**, was founded around 926 by Prince Wenceslas who, with his martyrdom at the hands of his brother Boleslav the Cruel in 935, was made patron saint of Bohemia and protector of the whole Czech nation. Initially intended to serve the needs of the Přemyslid princes, it became the seat of Prague's bishops when the town was raised to a bishopric in 973. It was not long before the small rotunda had to be enlarged to serve the needs of a burgeoning royal community and in 1060, instigated by Prince Spytihněv II (1055-1061), building started on a new triple naved basilica. Remnants from the excavations of these two early structures are preserved in the antechambers of the Royal Burial Vault which may be entered via the staircase in the Chapel of the Holy Cross.
When Charles IV succeeded in raising the status of Prague to an archbishopric in 1344, he founded the Cathedral of St. Vitus, summoning the French architect Mathieu d'Arras to plan and initiate the project. By the time of his death in 1352, Arras had completed only the choir ambulatory with its eight polygonal chapels, and it was

St. Vitus: the tympanum of the West Door.

St. Vitus: the West Door

left to the innovatory genius of Peter Parler of Gmund to continue the work, reshaping the original designs with his own keen instinct for the principles of late Gothic architecture. He modified the polygonal chapels into square ones, enlarged the Chapel of St. Wenceslas and made of it a unit separate from that of the choir proper. His also is the design of the south transept and tower along with the main southern portal, known as the Golden Gate from the red and gold ground of the mosaic of the Last Judgement set into the facade. This elaborate representation, the work of a team of Italian mosaicists working around 1370, depicts the patron saints of Bohemia grouped beneath the central figure of Christ enthroned. Kneeling below in the spandrels of the central arch, hands clasped in solemn supplication, are the figures of Charles IV himself with his consort Elizabeth of Pomerania. By 1385 the east end of the Cathedral was completed and Parler's sons finished off the main steeple to the height of the later Renaissance parapet before 1406. Thereafter the best part of five hundred years were to pass before any major advances in the construction process were made. The Hussite Wars brought a halt to the westerly development of the

athedral and the Neo-Gothic nave, the west facade and the west teeples were not completed until the end of the nineteenth century. 'he interior, however, does not hark of any great hiatus, the estrained Neo-Gothic nave directing the attention forward to the ltar and the powerful contrast between the shade of the ambulatory rcades and the resplendent flood of light through the clerestory. 'his is not meant to detract from the quality of the nave, whose ardy addition allowed some of the greatest of Prague's nineteenth-entury artists and glass craftsmen to collaborate on the strikingly eautiful scheme of stained and painted glass windows, through hich the light throws myriad shafts, dappling the paving slabs with mpid colour. The most beautiful of these is the extraordinary Art Jouveau window (third chapel on the left from the West Door), epicting scenes from the lives of Saints Cyril and Methodius, by lfons Mucha. Although Mucha was born in Prague, he spent much f his time in Paris where he was perhaps best known for his series f posters of Sarah Bernhardt.

)f all the Gothic chapels set around the east end and choir, by far ne most venerated is that of **St. Wenceslas**. Richly adorned with

St. Vitus: view along the nave.

Page 78
Construction work on St. Vitus started here at the east end.

Page 79
St. Vitus: Alfons Mucha's stunning painted window in the New Archbishop's Chapel.

BANKA
SLAVIE

The Coronation Crown of Charles IV in the St. Vitus Treasury.

Legend has it that St. Wenceslas clung to this ring at his martyrdom.

Gothic murals and inlaid with precious stones set into gold plaster i the Byzantine tradition, it is both an embodiment of the convergenc of the eastern and western arms of Christianity and a tribute to the dominance of the latter under the guidance of Bohemia's most popular saint. A copy of the lion's head door ring to which Wenceslas clung while his brother Boleslav laid on mercilessly with his sword is attached to the door of the chapel.

Opposite the monument of Count Schlick, to the right of the choir, is the Chapel of the Holy Cross which gives access to the **Royal Burial Vault**. Here, enshrouded in granite and pewter sarcophagi, ar preserved the remains of some of the Luxemburg dynasty of kings, including Charles IV and his son Wenceslas, along with those of the Habsburgs who made Prague their royal residence, Rudolf II and Maria Theresa. The exit brings us out in front of the late Renaissance white marble **Imperial Mausoleum**, bearing reliefs on th upper panel of Emperor Ferdinand I, his consort Anna Jagiello and his son Maximilian. On the lateral panels are depicted portraits of Charles IV and his four wives together with those of George of Poděbrady and Ladislav Posthumous. The sculptural decoration of the ground floor was devoted in the first instance to the past history of the Premyslid kings, the chapels bearing six tombs of Premyslid rulers. The triforium, however, is composed of twenty-one portrait busts, not only of members of the Luxemburg dynasty but also of Prague archbishops, the Master of Works and the two architects of the Gothic part of the Cathedral. The fact that commoners are presented alongside royalty and high ranking members of the clergy points towards the cult of the individual that was to become such ar important precept of humanism and the Renaissance.

On either side of the high altar are positioned two wooden relief

rvings, by K. Bendl, from the first quarter of the seventeenth ntury. Looking towards the east end, the one on the left of the gh altar depicts the Flight of the Winter King, Frederick V of the latinate after the Battle of the White Mountain. With its view of e Old Town, Charles Bridge and Malá Strana it provides an eresting architectural record of the city before the calamities of e Thirty Years War. When Emperor Matthias died in the spring of 19 he should have been succeeded by his nephew Ferdinand absburg. The Protestant Bohemian Estates had other ideas, wever, and rejected him in favour of Frederick, who they saw as a otestant sympathiser. They had good reason to believe that ederick would aid them in their cause, firstly because of his sition at the head of the Union of German Protestants and condly because of his marriage to Elizabeth, daughter of the nglish King James I, a vehement anti-Catholic. Frederick fortunately proved to be weak and ineffectual, his reign lasting but year before the snubbed Ferdinand, at the head of the joint armies Bavaria and Saxony, returned to defeat the Bohemian Estates at e Battle of the White Mountain in 1620.

St. Wenceslas Chapel.

George and Martin of Cluj: St. George and the Dragon (1373). The earliest piece of free-standing bronze sculpture in Central Europe. National Gallery, St. George Convent.

Detail from the silver Tomb of St. John Nepomuk.

The Bohemian Chancellery, site of the Second Defenestration of Prague in 1618.

On the right of the High Altar, just beyond the second wooden rel panel which depicts a view of the city from about 1630, is the sumptuously wrought silver **Tomb of St. John of Nepomuk**. This exuberant and costly tomb, made in Vienna in 1733-36, reflects jus how important the ubiquitous figure of the recently canonized saint was for the cause of the Catholic monarchic autocracy.

Outside, positioned roughly in the centre of the third courtyard, is copy of a statue representing another saint who played a prominent part in the Czech hagiography, especially up here in the Castle precinct. Although sections of it were recast at the end of the sixteenth century, the statue of St. George and the Dragon (the original forms part of the National Gallery's collection installed nearby in the Convent of St. George) by George and Martin of Cl is the oldest piece of free-standing Gothic bronze sculpture in Central Europe.

Beyond this, at the east end of the square, a small flight of steps leads up to the entrance to the **Old Royal Palace**. Deep in its bowe are preserved chambers from some of the earliest construction perio of the original fortifications, including the Soběslav Palace and part of the ninth-century curtain walls. The central focus on this level, however, is provided by the enormous expanse of the **Vladislav Hal** which at sixty-two metres in length, sixteen metres in width and rising to a height of thirteen metres, is by far the largest secular interior from this period in Prague. With its noble proportions and the intricacies of the reticulated Lierne vaulting it also ranks as one of the most beautiful. Built by Benedikt Ried between 1493 and 1503, it was here that the Bohemian kings were elected, and the walls once rang with the sound of hooves at the gallop when tournaments were actually held inside the palace. A special **Riders'** taircase, entering the Hall about two thirds along the left hand wall, ·as incorporated into the design for this very purpose. In the south-·est corner of the Hall is the entrance to the chambers of the **ohemian Chancellery**, the outermost of which was the scene of the econd Defenestration in 1618, when three aberrant governors were ırown out of the east window. Looking out of this window for a ıoment towards the exterior wall of the Vladislav Hall, the earliest lements of the Italian Renaissance to be incorporated in the rchitecture of Prague are visible in the rectangular, pilastered ·indow linings that adorn the facade. At the east end of the Hall a ight of steps leads up into the oratory of **All Saints Chapel**, an arlier structure (1370-87) by Peter Parler, built to service the needs f the convent for noble ladies which was sited to the east of the)ld Royal Palace. Also included amongst the chambers that open off ıe Vladislav Hall are the late Gothic **Hall of the Diet** in the north-ast corner, and the **New Appeal Court** to the west of the Riders' taircase, which exits onto St. George's Square. This is undoubtedly ne of the most picturesque areas contained within the Castle walls. orded to the south by the walls of the Church of All Saints and ıose of the Vladislav Hall, the space is presided over by the ıagisterial, russet facade of the **Basilica of St. George**. 'his church, apart from being the oldest in Hradčany, is the best

Following page
The imposing interior of Vladislav's Great Hall in the Old Royal Palace.

The Baroque façade of St. George's Church. The oldest surviving church in Prague.

Left
The early Romanesque interior of the Church of St. George.

Master Theodoric: St. Jerome (before 1365). National Gallery, Convent of St. George.

:eserved example of Romanesque architecture not only in Prague ıt also in the whole of Bohemia. The facade is Baroque but the hite towers that rise behind with their double orders of omanesque arches beckon us to explore further. The church was unded as early as 912 by Duke Vratislav I, giving rise to the tablishment of the adjacent convent, the first in Bohemia, in 937. he east towers were added after a fire in 1142 and shortly terwards the lower part of the Chapel of St. Ludmila (Wenceslas's andmother) was built on to the south tower. The church was ırther modified towards the end of the seventeenth century when it as given its present facade, but thanks to extensive archaeological search followed by a reconstruction programme the church has now ad its original Romanesque appearance faithfully restored. The eighbouring convent contains a permanent exhibition of trends in ohemian painting from the Gothic through to the Baroque. xceptional amongst these are the bold portraits by Master heodoric and the Crucifixion scenes by other masters whose names e not known, which reveal the persistent fascination with the Blood

Fourteenth century Bohemian Master: St. Vitus Madonna and Child. National Gallery, Convent of St. George.

Karel Škréta: Portrait of the gem cutter Dionysio Miseroni and family (1653). National Gallery, Convent of St. George.

Master of the Třebon Altar: Resurrection (before 1380). National Gallery, Convent of St. George.

Master of the Rajhrad Altar: Crucifixion (before 1420). National Gallery, Convent of St. George.

N° 22 Golden Lane: Franz Kafka lived and worked here. The Golden Lane at Prague Castle.

of Christ that was to prove central to the divergence of the Utraquists from the liturgy of the Roman Catholic Church.
Any tour of Hradčany should include a visit to the tiny street of fairytale houses known as the **Golden Lane** (Zlatá ulička), which line the northern wall of the castle beyond the east end of the Basilica of St. George. Legend has it that this is where Rudolf II installed his band of alchemists, but in fact it is now known that their workshops and laboratories were housed in the **Mihulkar Powder Tower** on Vikářská, where there is now an exhibition of some of the equipmen they used in their experiments. These miniature houses were actually built by members of the palace guard who plied various trades at times when their armed services were not required. Today they are occupied on the whole by gift shops.

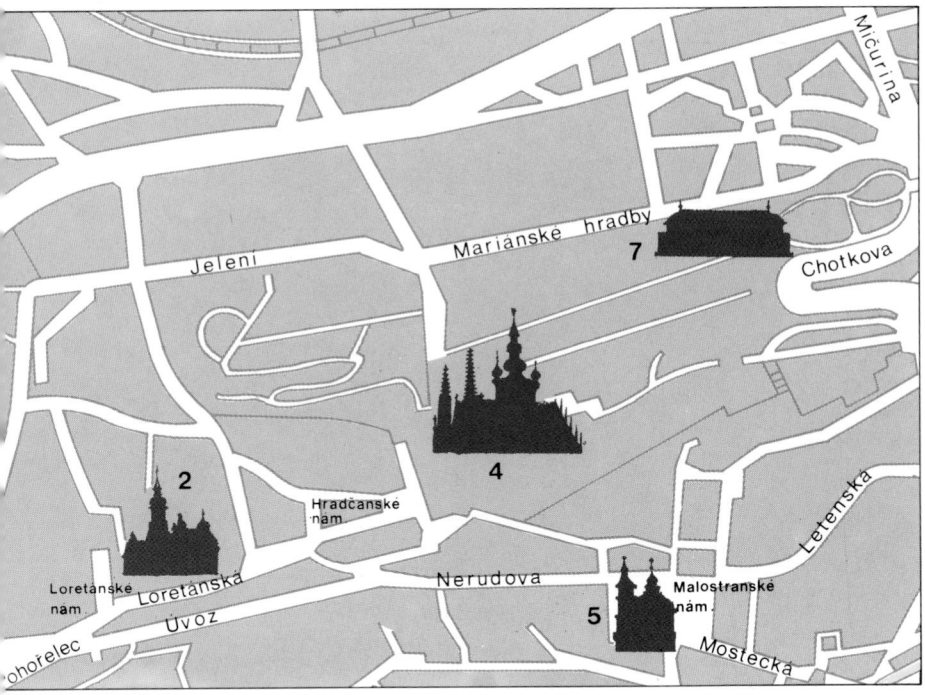

RADČANY SQUARE AND NOVÝ SVĚT

1320 a third Prague settlement was founded by the Castle's rgrave, Berka of Duba. Originally intended as a town for serfs, its ildings were laid out on a site taking up about half the area of the esent Hradčany Square. During the fourteenth century the town s considerably extended by Charles IV to include the areas of oz, Pohořelec and Nový Svět, thereby filling in the gap between e Hradčany fortifications and those of the Strahov Monastery. owever, despite its scale, the town was denied municipal lependence for over two hundred and fifty years and therefore, e to its complete dependence on the castle, was considerably less portant than either Malá Strana or the Old Town. The great fire ich raged in Malá Strana and Hradčany in 1541 decimated the a, leaving the way clear for those nobles who wished to enhance eir status and bring it to the attention of the neighbouring royals develop Hradčany Square and skirt it with the large palaces which nain to the present day. The first of these was the **Schwarzenberg lace** on the south side which now commands the top of Nerudova, massive walls scored with diamond sgraffito in the style of the lian Renaissance. On the opposite side of the square stands the er Baroque **Palace of the Archbishops of Prague** which, to the nsternation of some tourists, completely conceals the buildings of e **Sternberg Palace**, now housing collections from the National allery of Prague. Access to this palace and its galleries may be ined through the unassuming arch on the far left of the facade of e Archbishop's Palace.

aving the square to the west via Kanovnická takes us past the autiful **Martinic Palace** (No. 8/67), once more delicately adorned th sgraffito scenes from the Bible including King David and the ight of Joseph from Potiphar. This narrow street, following the

The magnificent Schwarzenberg Palace.

natural lines of the hillocks beyond Hradčany and struck through with a timeless, serene peace, runs into **Nový Svět** (New World), th heart of the former poor quarter. Although it is known that Dvořák New World symphony was inspired by a trip to the United States, the sleepy solitude of these streets is immediately redolent of its mournful, long-suffering but stately theme. Taking a left into Černínská at the end of Nový Svět leads us up into Loreto Square,the scene of an unequal duel between the daunting, diamond rusticated bulk of the **Černín Palace** and the peaceable centre of pilgrimage opposite, the **Loreto**, armed only with the exquisite peal of bells from her late seventeenth-century carillon. Behind K. I. Dientzenhofer's Baroque facade is encircled the Santa Casa Shrine, modelled on the one at Loreto in Italy, which according to the legend was the house of the Virgin Mary, transferred there from the Holy Land. About fifty of these shrines were built in Bohemia, as part of the concerted attempt by the Counter-Reformation to enhance the appeal of Catholicism to ordinary people. But they were also popular amongst the pilgrims of the nobility who made precious votive offerings of quite extraordinary value, including the renownec

Right
Albrecht Dürer: Feast of the Rose Garlands (1506). National Gallery, Sternberg Palace.

Lucas Cranach the Elder: Virgin and Child with Saints Catherine and Barbara (1510-1520). National Gallery, Sternberg Palace.

The Archbishop's Palace.

Left
The tranquility of Nový Svět.

Martinic Palace.

The imposing façade of the Černín Palace.

Loreto: The Clock Tower with its seventeenth-century carillon.

Entrance to the Loreto and its Santa Casa shrine.

Left
The garden façade of Černín Palace.

Diamond Monstrance, from the Loreto Treasury.

Diamond Monstrance (c. 1699, Vienna), exhibited upstairs in the Loreto Treasury.

Pohořelec runs west from the far end of the square towards the **Strahov Monastery** whose twin spires topped with onion domes dominate the northern slopes of Petřín Hill. Founded in 1140 by Vladislav II, it is the oldest Premonstratensian monastery in Bohemi and was originally fortified because until the construction of the Hunger Wall in about 1320, it lay outside the fortifications of Hradčany. Here, over the centuries, the brothers amassed a staggering quantity of illustrated manuscripts and books so that by the end of the eighteenth century the collection included volumes

Right
The spires of Strahov from the Castle ramp.

Strahov Monastery: The Philosophical Hall.

containing very nearly the entire literary output of western Christianity. Small wonder then that when the Czech State dissolved all religious orders in Czechoslovakia in 1952, incorporating their collections into the monastery library, they had in the Strahov a ready-made Museum of National Literature, which is the purpose it serves today. The Old Library, which even before the dissolution

Strahov Monastery: the Theological Hall.

ontained in the region of 130,000 volumes, now comprises a nammoth 900,000 books, as well as 5,000 illuminated manuscripts. However, the central focus of its exhibition is formed by the ollections installed in the **Theological Hall** and the adjacent **Philosophical Hall**, situated in the building to the right of the Baroque Church of the Assumption (Kostel Nanebevzetí Panny Marie).

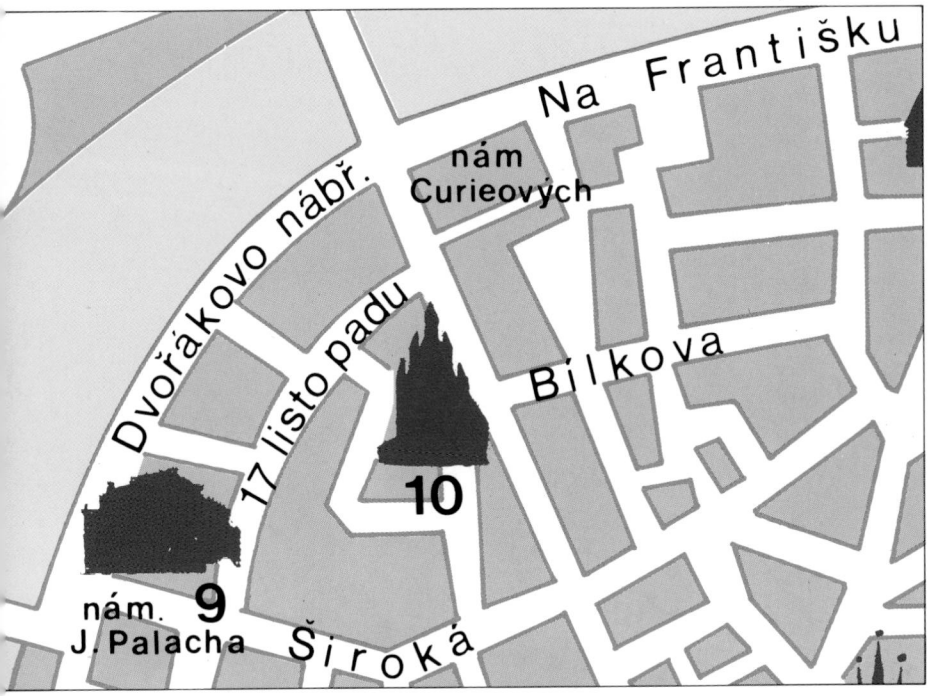

OSEFOV, THE FORMER PRAGUE GHETTO

'he Jews were early settlers in Prague. Ever vigilant for those areas kely to reap the profits of international trade, they were among the rst aliens to realize the rich future that Prague had in store, due to 's position on the main east-west trade route. Their original ommunities sprang up around the beginning of the tenth century in ne Malá Strana, in the area now known as Újezd, and beneath the 'yšehrad on the opposite bank of the Vltava. During the thirteenth entury there was a gradual expansion from these early settlements nto the vicinity of the present-day Old New Synagogue. The Jews nat populated the narrow winding alleys between the Old Town quare and the bend of the Vltava were segregated from the 'hristian community not only by the philosophical differences of neir creed, but also by the physical barrier of a wall. This had been uilt in accordance with the edict of the Third Lateran Council 179), which stated that areas inhabited by Jews should be separated rom the dwellings of Christians by a fence, wall or moat.

n the first instance, therefore, the term Jewish Town indicated not ne administrative autonomy of the area, but rather the first step wards the ghettoizing process of the sixteenth century, when any ncoming Jews were compulsorily settled in the district. This ghetto nderwent a significant expansion during the seventeenth century so nat by the time of the Habsburg Kings Maximilian and Rudolf II, nere were probably as many as seven thousand Jews packed into 'hat must have become a network of narrow, squalid and unhygienic nes. The conditions became so horrendous that even the distracted udolf lent an ear to the proposals of his finance minister Mordechaj Markus Maisl, who subsequently arranged for the repaving of the hetto, the construction of the Jewish Town Hall and the Maisl ynagogue, and established the Old Jewish cemetery. Maislova, the

Left
The Jewish Town Hall and the Old New Synagogue.

Preceeding pages
The Old New Synagogue.

The Old New Synagogue and the monument to Moses.

street in which the eponymous Synagogue stands, was named in memory of his philanthropic redevelopment.
Much of the old Jewish Town was demolished during slum clearances at the end of the nineteenth century when the new buildings were laid out around the straight and largely characterless street of Pařížská. However, the core buildings of the religious community were preserved even through the Nazi occupation, when Hitler had intended to found a museum to an extinct race here in Prague. Some of the artefacts that he collected from synagogues all over Europe for that very purpose are preserved here in the buildings of the Jewish State Museum.
About three quarters of the way up Pařížská, on the left, we come to the **Old New Synagogue**. (Tickets for all the exhibitions of the Jewish State Museum may be purchased from the High Synagogue, opposite the entrance to the Old New Synagogue in Červená).
The Old New Synagogue is one of the first Gothic structures in Prague. The oldest part dates back to the mid-thirteenth century, making it the oldest preserved synagogue in Europe. Originally consisting only of a barrel vaulted lower chamber, the building was enlarged by the construction of a double aisled hall in the last quarter of the century, thereby creating the space necessary to hold separate services for men and women. The only time when Jewish men and women are permitted to worship together is during the wedding ceremony. The proportions and decoration inside are governed by the number twelve, symbolizing the twelve tribes of Israel. The benches lining the walls are late Empire and are still used in the services today. There is one seat, however, that no one is allowed to use. This is due to the fact that this seat, situated to the right of the altar, belonged to the legendary Rabbi Löwe.
Rabbi Löwe was a leading figure in the Jewish community during the reign of Rudolf II, best remembered now for his association with the ancient mystical creature — the Golem. Legend has it that he created the Golem in the dead of night from the clay and mud on the banks of the Vltava. The creature would lie dormant until the Shem (a Hebrew magic word) was uttered and the sign of life was placed in his mouth. With that the Golem was animated and became charged with the mission of going out into the community, discovering crimes and preventing them. Perhaps it was the Golem that persuaded Rudolf to do something about the appalling conditions in the ghetto. All went well until one evening before the Sabbath when Rabbi Löwe forgot to remove the sign of life from the mouth of the Golem. Even mythical monsters need a day off and the creature thus denied fell into an orgy of destruction in the Rabbi's house. The Rabbi, alerted by the commotion, found the Golem, deactivated him by chanting another Shem and then removed the sign of life from the creature's mouth. With this, the monster turned back into clay and mud and was finally laid to rest beneath the roof timbers of the Old New Synagogue.
On the corner of Červená and Maislova is situated the **Jewish Town Hall**, built in the late sixteenth century with funding from Mayor M Maisl as an administrative centre. Although this recognized a certain degree of autonomy, it was not until 1850 that the Jewish Town

The Neo-Romanesque cemetery house.

became a separate quarter of the city and was renamed Josefov in memory of Emperor Joseph II. Crossing over Maislova, head down the street called U starého hřbitova towards the Neo-Romanesque turreted building which guards the entrance to the Old Jewish Cemetery. On the left as the street bends sharply to the right is the **Klaus Synagogue**, housing an exhibition of Hebrew manuscripts and old prints, including one of Tycho de Brahe with his silver nose. The building to the right of the entrance to the **Old Jewish Cemetery** houses a rather harrowing display of drawings by the children of Terezín concentration camp.

The cemetery is one of the most bizarre and stirring sights in Prague. There are over ten thousand bodies piled one on top of the other here, beneath the grey disarray of tombstones which lean toward the ground like teeth rocking in decaying gums. Coffins were not used, the bodies being simply wrapped in muslin, thereby facilitating the stacking process. Small pebbles placed in rows along every available edge of the stones supplant the Christian tradition of adorning graves with flowers. Also unlike Christian practice, where one tombstone

Gravestones in the Old Jewish Cemetery.

ight mark the resting place of a whole family, here there is a separate one for every person, except for children under the age of one. mong the celebrated figures of the Jewish community buried here are huda Ben Bezalel, the famous Rabbi Löwe, Mordechaj Maisl, the ayor of the Jewish town, the physician and physicist, Josef elmedigo, and the connoisseur of the Talmud David Oppenheimer. he stones are inscribed with symbols that relate to the name or ofession of the deceased. The grave of Rabbi Löwe, for example, ars the symbol of the lion, which is the meaning of his surname in erman. Alternatively, the symbol of crossed hands is reserved for ose with connections with priestly or Levite families. An aristocratic at-of-arms is to be found on the gravestone of Hindel Basevi, calling the fact that she was the wife of the first Prague Jew to be ised to the nobility. Through the trees to the south-west sits the othic, single-naved Pinkas Synagogue which now serves as a emorial to the 77,297 Bohemian and Moravian Jews who lost their ves in the Nazi gas chambers. Their names, 36,000 of them relating former citizens of Prague, are inscribed on the walls of the interior.

Jewish gravestones often portrayed a symbol relating either to the name or the profession of the deceased.

The wall in the Pinkas Synagogue bearing the names of those Jews who perished in Nazi concentration camps.

The tomb of Rabbi Löwe.

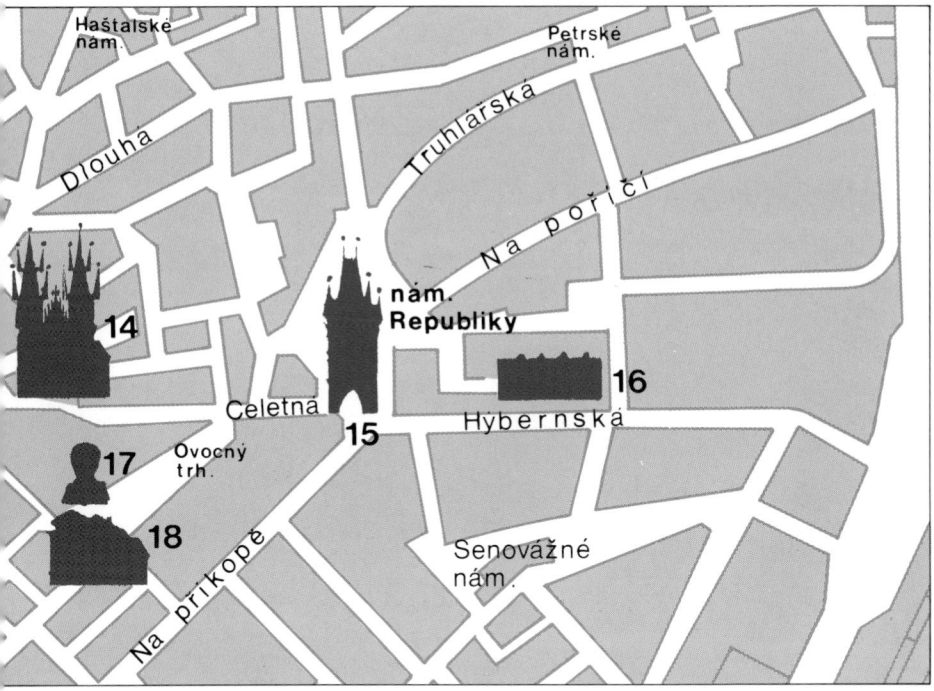

'OVÉ MĚSTO - THE NEW TOWN

ıe New Town was founded by Charles IV in 1348 to create extra arket space and to house the increasing number of craftsmen drawn Prague by the city's blossoming economy. The scale of its nception was quite remarkable with strict regulations laid down verning the standard of construction work and completion clauses ıilt into the contracts, stating that work had to commence within a onth and be completed within a year and a half. Similar impetus as given to the construction of the town's fortifications which after ıly two years ran for almost three kilometres, containing the plots id out between the Old Town and the Castle at Vyšehrad. Today ıly the section running from here up to the Church of Our Lady ıd Charlemagne at Karlov remain, but they are imposing enough to mind us of the power and influence that the mediaeval city ıjoyed.

ıe commercial heart of the New Town was centred around two ain squares whose dimensions, even to the modern eye, are quite aggering. **Wenceslas Square** (Václavské náměstí) is 680 metres long ıd 60 metres wide. Although it has the appearance today of a large ɔulevard, and architecturally nothing has survived from its Gothic yday, its bustling jam of shoppers denoting it as the consumer ntre of contemporary Prague can't be very much different from the owds that would have gathered here when it functioned as harles's great Horse Market. Apart from the few remaining Art ouveau facades, such as that of the beautiful Hotel Europa and the rly twentieth-century equestrian statue of St. Wenceslas, there is tle of any great artistic interest remaining in the Square. Even the amatic buildings of the Neo-Classical National Museum (1885-90) em slovenly and overbearing, which, given the immensity of the uare they close, is really saying something. The architect of the

Following page Wenceslas Square.

INTER

DIVADLO

HÔTEL
GRAND HOTEL EUROPA

Hotel Evropa: light fittings in the coffee bar.

roject, Josef Schulz, also assisted on the construction of the slightly arlier National Theatre at the end of Narodní, next to the Bridge of egions. But this is a far more successful attempt at creating a Neo-enaissance building and a fitting symbol of the Czech nation's etermination to provide itself with its own cultural milieu. Prior to his, Prague's theatres, including the Tyl in the Old Town, were erman run and catered exclusively for a German-speaking audience. n 1845 a request for funding to build a new Czech Theatre was ejected by the now German dominated Estates. In response a ationwide appeal was launched to raise the necessary finance: the ite was purchased and in 1881 the National Theatre opened with its irst performance of Smetana's *Libuše*. Only two months later the ewly completed Theatre was burned down, but it is a testament to he Czech people's resolve to provide their nation with this facility hat it was rebuilt and reopened within two years.

Overall, very little remains from the period of the town's foundation. This is the result partly of the fact that the New Town, which oused the largest proportion of the city's poor, was the seedbed and tronghold of the Hussite radicals and therefore suffered to a greater xtent from the reprisals of the anti-reform movement. There are, owever, two churches founded at the same time as the town which ave survived, albeit with certain modifications, down to the present. t the northern end of the square a small arcade cuts through into ungmann Square where we find, secreted behinded an uninspiring loister wall, the remarkable peace provided by the **Church of St.**

Left
Hotel Evropa. After Paris and Vienna, Prague was the main centre for Art Nouveau and Secession.

MUSEUM · REGNI · BOHEMIAE
VACLAV · II.
RUDOLF · II.

Mary of the Snows. The name alone betokens the serenity of the building founded in 1347 as a monastic church for the Royal Coronation. The interior proportions of the church feel quite odd, the nave being so high in relation to its length that one could almost imagine oneself in the base of a huge tower. This is because the church was originally intended to be much larger, surpassing even St. Vitus Cathedral in size. However due to lack of funds and the interruption caused by the Hussite Wars, the building was never completed to plan, so that what we are left with now is a church made solely from the presbytery of the structure which was to have stretched the hundred metres to Jungmann Square itself. Situated right on the outskirts of Charles's New Town is the extraordinary **Church of the Assumption and Charles the Great** (Kostel Nanebevzetí Panny Marie a Karla Velikého). Construction started in 1358 on an octagonal plan based on that of Charlemagne's Palatine Chapel in Aachen and the church was consecrated in 1377. Although one can still imagine the essence of the Gothic building, especially in Wolmut's late sixteenth-century restoration of the ribbed stellar vaulting, the dome which marks it out from afar is the result of Baroque modifications.

The administrative centre of the New Town was the **New Town Hall** which still stands on Charles Square — the former Cattle Market. This was the scene for the act that sparked the turbulent period of the Hussite Wars. On 22nd July 1419, Jan Želivský, a Hussite radical, stormed the Town Hall at the head of an angry mob, demanding the release of fellow Hussites imprisoned in the buildings. When the councillors refused to comply with their demands, two of them were hurled from the window in what became known as the First Defenestration of Prague.

Charles Square, 530 metres in length by 150 metres in width, is the largest square in Prague. Today, however, its dimensions are deceptive, the area having been planted as parkland in the middle of the nineteenth century, at around the same time that the entire New Town underwent a wholesale redevelopment. It is still a good place to head to just for a wander and to sit and listen to the romantic rumble of trams as they course round the square, heading for all four corners of the city.

The Baroque **Church of St. Ignatius**, which dominates the square at the point where it is intersected by Ječná and Resslova, formed the centre of the Jesuit mission in the New Town along with the immense adjacent Jesuit College, surpassed in scale only by the Clementinum. A short distance away in Resslova stand two churches worthy of attention. The first, the Baroque **Church of Saints Cyril and Methodius**, is remembered as the last hiding place of the Czech resistance fighters responsible for the assassination of Reinhard Heydrich in 1942. Having succesfully completed their mission they were cornered by the Nazis in the crypt of the church where they held out for some time before being overcome and shot.

As a reprisal, the Nazis razed the outlying village of Lidice to the ground, executing all the men over the age of sixteen and deporting the women and children to concentration camps. A memorial tablet bearing the names of those who died in the crypt recalls the courage

The National Museum.

Following page
The National Theatre.

nd heroism of their last days. Across the road stands the Gothic **Church of St. Wenceslas** in Zderaz. Originally a Romanesque church, lements of which are preserved in the west wall, it served the small ommunity of Zderaz which was subsequently incorporated into the ayout of the New Town. On a site slightly to the west of the church, n Dittrichova, there originally stood a small castle, built for the use of Venceslas IV in about 1399. The bath building in the southernmost ortion of the castle existed through to the end of the nineteenth entury and was the scene in 1848 of a meeting called by the Czech Repeal which led ultimately to the revolution of the same year. Returning to Charles Square, head for Vyšehradská which makes an xit in the south west. On the corner on the left as we leave the quare stands the originally Renaissance building known from the eventeenth century as the **Faustus House**. The legend of a man who old his soul to the Devil for the temporal gratification of his body riginated in Germany in the late sixteenth century, but swiftly gained opularity all through northern Europe.

The special quality of Prague, with her long history of multiracial co-xistence complemented by a corresponding architectural eclecticism, is ot easily forgotten. Czechs, Germans, Austrians, Italians and renchmen have all left their mark in the cultural palimpsest of the ity. Prague is indeed a "threshold," not only to Central and Eastern urope but to new and vital experience.

The National Theatre: Proscenium arch and boxes.

Left
The stairwell of the National Museum.

CHRONOLOGY

c850 - 895 The Czech tribes are conquered by Duke Bořivoj, the first historically attested member of the Premyslid dynasty, who initiates the construction of Hradčany Castle.

874 Methodius, the Apostle of the Slavs, baptises Bořivoj. After his death his Christian wife, Ludmila, is murdered thereby becoming Bohemia's first martyr and patron saint.

900 - 1000 Jewish, German, French and Italian merchants settle in Prague.

921 Ludmila's grandson, Wenceslas, becomes Duke of Bohemia and builds the Rotunda of St. Vitus.

935 Wenceslas murdered by his brother Boleslav the Cruel.

973 Prague is elevated to the status of bishopric and Adalbert is invested as the first incumbent to the episcopal see.

993 Adalbert founds the Benedictine Abbey at Břevnov.

995 Premyslid domination is consolidated with the assassination of the Slavniks, the second most powerful family in Bohemia.

1085 Duke Vratislav II is crowned as the first King of Bohemia, a title granted to him by Emperor Henry V in gratitude for his assistance with the struggle for the investiture of Pope Gregory VII.

1140 Vladislav II founds the premonstratensian monastery at Strahov.

1158 Duke Vladislav II is awarded the hereditary title of King by Emperor Frederick Barbarossa in appreciation of his assistance against rebellious Northern Italian towns.

1170 Construction work starts on the Judith Bridge, the first stone bridge across the Vltava.

1178 Duke Soběslav II grants German merchants certain privileges as encouragement for them to stay in Prague. These include the right to be dealt with by German Law, tax incentives and exemption from military service.

1198 The Emperor raises Přemysl Otakar I to the status of King.

1231 Under Wenceslas I the Old Town receives its municipal charter and is fortified with walls.

1232 - 1234 Eberhard, later to be Master of the Royal Mint, founds the Gall Town within the precinct of the Old Town walls.

1257 The area now known as Malá Strana is established by Přemysl Otakar II as a German settlement governed by the Magdeburg legal code.

1306 The Premyslid dynasty dies out with the murder of Wenceslas III.

310 After four turbulent years, during which the Habsburgs attempted unsuccesfully to take the throne of Bohemia for the first time, John of Luxemburg, husband to the Premyslid princess Elizabeth, fights his way into the city and becomes King.

1320 Berka of Dubé, the Burgrave of Prague Castle, founds a third town along the old road from Pohořelec to the castle and names it Hradčany.

338 John of Luxemburg grants the inhabitants of the Old Town the right to build their own Town Hall in return for their financing of his foreign campaigns.

344 Charles IV rules Bohemia as regent. Thanks to his benign relationship with the Holy See, he manages to raise Prague to an archbishopric and founds the Cathedral of St. Vitus.

346 Charles IV becomes King of Bohemia.

348 Charles founds his eponymous university together with the New Town which makes Prague the largest city in Central Europe.

355 Charles becomes Holy Roman Emperor and Prague is raised to the capital city of the Holy Roman Empire.

357 Charles builds a new stone bridge to replace the Judith bridge that had been swept away by a flood in 1342.

360 Charles extends Malá Strana in a southerly direction and encloses it within a new wall.

378 - 1419 During the weak reign of Wenceslas IV social unrest increases with a decline in the moral standards of the clergy.

409 Prompted by Jan Hus, Wenceslas alters the voting structure within the university with the Decree of Kutná Hora, thereby giving the native Bohemians a distinct advantage over the Germans, many of whom leave the country in disgust.

415 Jan Hus is summoned to the Council of Constance to defend his "heretical" views on the teaching of the Church. Refusing to retract his beliefs, he is burned at the stake despite having been guaranteed safe passage, thereby sparking off a vociferous, countrywide reaction to the established Church.

419 A crowd led by Jan Želivský storms the New Town Hall demanding the release of imprisoned Hussite radicals. The councillors refuse and are hurled to their deaths from the windows in what became known as the First Defenestration of Prague.

420 Pope Martin V issues a Papal Bull proclaiming a crusade against heretics in Bohemia, thereby instigating the period of the Hussite Wars. Between 1421 and 1431 a total of five crusades are launched against the Hussites by the combined forces of the Empire, all of which ended in humiliating defeat for the Holy Armies.

1436 - 71 George of Poděbrady emerges from the turmoil of the Hussite conflict and is elected King. In his desire to uphold the Compacts of Basle, which held the divergent Utraquists in a fragile peace with Rome, he was forced to play a skilful game of cut and thrust diplomacy, through which he secured the Bohemian succession for the friendly, Jagiellan dynasty in Poland.

1490 The domains of the Bohemian crown are united with those of Poland and Hungary as King Vladislav Jagiello transfers the capital from Prague to Buda.

1526 Ferdinand Habsburg is elected King of Bohemia, thereby establishing the dominion of the mighty Austrian family which was to last right up to 1918.

1541 Renaissance rebuilding of Prague takes place after a devastating fire in Hradčany and Malá Strana.

1549 onwards The impetus of the Counter-Reformation, introduced into Bohemia by the Habsburgs, is tempered by the settling in Prague of a community of German Lutherans.

1556 Ferdinand I becomes Emperor and invites the Jesuits to Prague as missionaries for the Catholic conversion of the populace.

1575 The Bohemian non Catholic religious factions — predominantly the Neo-Utraquists, the Czech Brethren and the Lutherans — agree on the Czech Confession which was to replace the outmoded Compacts of Basle.

1583-1612 Czech culture profits from the temporary transfer of the Imperial Court from Vienna to Prague, which under Rudolf II becomes a centre for artistic and intellectual endeavour unparalleled since the days of Charles IV.

1609 In the face of overwhelming opposition from the Estates and his brother Matthias Corvinus in Hungary, Rudolf II finally capitulates and signs the Letter of Majesty, granting religious freedom to the Bohemians.

1611 On the abdication of Rudolf II, his brother Matthias becomes King.

1618 Catholic officials deliberately violate the terms of Rudolf's Letter of Majesty. In retribution they are thrown from the windows of the Bohemian Chancellery by members of the radical Protestant nobility in what became known as the Second Defenestration of Prague. This action results ultimately in the Thirty Years War.

1619 The Bohemian Estates reject the succession of Matthias's nephew Ferdinand II and choose instead Frederick V, Elector of the Palatinate, as King.

1620 Ferdinand II returns to Prague to claim his throne and utterly defeats the forces of the Bohemian Estates at the Battle of the White Mountain. Frederick V, known as the "Winter King" after his pitifully short reign, flees the city.

621 Twenty-seven leaders of the Protestant anti-Habsburg uprising are executed on the Old Town Square.

627 The Catholic faith becomes the only permissible religion. Those members of the nobility who refuse to adopt the Catholic faith are forced to emigrate leaving all their property behind, thereby reducing the population of Bohemia by one quarter.

631 During the course of the Thirty Years War the Swedish army has advanced to the gates of Prague but is driven back by General Albrecht Wallenstein.

648 The Peace of Westphalia seals the end of the Thirty Years War. Prague's economic and cultural importance diminishes rapidly.

741-42 Occupation of Prague by Franco-Bavarian forces.

781 Edict of Tolerance is passed by Joseph II. Programme of progressive reformation commences with the abolition of the monasteries.

784 The Old Town, New Town, Hradčany and Malá Strana are united as a single administrative whole.

848 An unsuccessful Czech nationalist uprising in the streets of Prague follows the authorities' refusal to grant equal rights for Czechs and Germans.

861 The February Constitution cedes certain powers to the democratically elected Empire Council.

882 Prague University is divided according to nationality.

918 The Czechoslovak Republic is established albeit with its borders unconfirmed. The subsequent incorporation of Slovakia and the Sudetenland was to have far reaching consequences for the Czechoslovak State.

938 In an atmosphere of appeasement the Munich Agreement is signed, thereby ceding the Sudetenland to Hitler's Germany.

939 Hitler incorporates the rest of the country into the Nazi Protectorate of Bohemia and Moravia.

945 The Czech government announces the Košice Programme for a socialist state, which, although it contained ideas similar to those expounded by President Beneš, was infused with communist content.

948 The Communist Party assumes power in a bloodless coup. Czechoslovakia becomes a People's Republic.

960 The Czechoslovak Socialist Republic is established.

968 The period of liberalisation under Svoboda and Dubček, known as the Prague Spring, is brought to a violent end by the intervention of Warsaw Pact troops.

989 On November 17th the people of Prague take to the streets and force the Central Council of the Communist Party to resign.

RESTAURANT LIST

Since the middle of the '90s, the number of restaurants that have opened in Prague ha increased on a more or less daily basis, to the point where it is now possible to find some where to suit just about anyone's taste and pocket.
Whether you want to try traditional Czech cuisine, Japanese sushi or dine out in a style tha would normally be more associated with London or Paris, you will find what you are look ing for in Prague's Old Town. The list of restaurants and pubs is endless, but set out belov are some of the best that can be found in the centre of the City. Note, though that ever day new places are opening and it is impossible to mention every highlight!
Whatever your taste, whilst you are in Prague you definitely should try the typical Czec cuisine which, although still based around meat and creamy sauces, is nowadays muc lighter than it was and will usually include fresh vegetables. If you like dumplings an lashings of gravy then you can't go far wrong with specialities of chicken or duck serve with red and white cabbage, or with the tempting palačinky – pancakes flambéed in alco hol and stuffed with fruit and ice cream.
Or, if you are looking for a special night out, try one of the international restaurants wher the food might be more to your taste, but where there is no mistaking that you are i Prague. One look out of the window at the River Vltava, with views of the Charles Bridg or the Castle and you will never want to leave!

CZECH
- U Modré Růže, Rytířská 16, Prague 1, 224 222 623
- U Modré Kachničky I., Nebovidská 6, Prague 1, 257 320 308
- U Modré Kachničky II., Michalská 16, Prague 1, 224 213 418
- David, Tržiště 21 /611, Prague 1
- U Vladaře, Maltézské nám. 10, Prague 1, 257 534 121
- U Mecenáše, Malostranské nám. 10, Prague 1, 257 531 631
- Kolkovna, V Kolkovně 8, Prague 1, 224 819 701
- Klub Architektů, Betlémské nám. 5a, Prague 1, 224 401 214
- U Kalicha, Na Bojišti 12-14, Prague 2, 224 912 557
- Novoměstský pivovar, Vodičkova 20, Prague 1, 222 231 662

ITALIAN
- Taverna Toscana, Michalská 23, Prague 1, 224 231 220
- Amici Miei, Vězeňská 5, Prague 1, 224 816 688
- Don Giovanni, Karolíny Světlé 34, Prague 1, 222 222 062
- Il Cardinale, Benediktská 3, Prague 1, 224 827 425

FRENCH
- Bistrot de Marlene, Plavecká 4, Prague 2, 224 921 853
- La Provence, Štupartská 9, Prague 1, 222 324 801
- Pallfy Palác, Valdštejnská 14, Prague 1, 257 530 522
- Pravda, Pařížská 17, Prague 1, 222 326 203
- Le Saint-Jacques, Jakubská 4, Prague 1, 222 322 685
- Chez Marcel, Haštalská 12, Prague 1, 222 315 676

JAPANESE
- Sushi Bar, Zborovská 49, Prague 1, 603 244 882
- Millhouse Sushi, Na Příkopě 22, Prague 1, 221 451 771
- Hanil, Slavíkova, Prague 3, 222 715 867

INDIAN
- Taj Mahal, Škrétova 10, Prague 1, 222 240 315
- Bombay, Dlouhá, Prague 1, 222 328 400

INTERNATIONAL
- Kampa Park, Na Kampě 8B, Prague 1, 257 532 685
- V Zátiší, Liliová 1, Prague 1, 222 221 155
- Mlýnec, Novotného Lávka 5, Prague 1, 221 082 208

AMERICAN
- Red Hot and Blues, Jakubská 12, Prague 1, 222 314 639
- Buffalo Bill's , Vodičkova 9, Prague 1, 224 948 624
- Kojak's , Anny Letenské 16, Prague 2, 222 250 594

LEBANESE
- Diwan, Savarin, Na Příkopě, Prague 1, 224 231 515

Rhapsody, Dukelských Hrdinů 46, Prague 7, 220 806 768

EAFOOD

La Cambusa, Klicperova 2, Prague 5, 602 374 189

Rybí Trh, Týn 5, Prague 1, 224 895 447

HINESE

China restaurant, Vodičkova 41, Prague 1, 224 152 540

Thanh Long, Ostrovní 23, Prague 1, 224 912 318

OSHER

King Solomon, Široká 8, Prague 1, 224 818 752

RENDY & FUNKY

Hergertova Cihelna, Cihelná 2B, Prague 1, 257 535 534

Square, Malostranské nám. 5, Prague 1, 257 532 109

La Provence, Štupartská 9, Prague 1, 222 324 801

Bazaar, Nerudova 40, Prague 1, 257 535 050

Hot, Wenceslas Square 43 (Václavské náměstí), Prague 1, 222 247 240

UBS AND BEER HALLS

rague beer halls are generally noisy, smelly places, but you won't care as they serve some f the best beer in the world such as Staropramen, Pilsen and Budvar. Or you might pre- er to taste an original local beer brewed in the restaurant you eat at, such as U Fleku or Novoměstský pivovar. There are no crushing queues for the bar as the beers are almost hrown at you where you sit, with prompt service that borders on the clairvoyant ensuring hat by the time you finish the first pint, the second will already be making its way across he room. With very relaxed opening and closing hours it is unwise to slip into a "pivnice" or a late drink as you may never leave!

EER HALLS

Malostranská pivnice, Cihelná 103/3, Prague 1, 257 530 032

U Vejvodů, Jilská 4/353, Prague 1, 224 210 591

U Pivrnce sportovce, Soukenická 1085/4, Prague 1, 224 816 609

Panok, Jungmannova 23/11, Prague 1, 224 946 776

U Fleků, Křemencova, Prague 1, 224 915 118

WINE BARS

lthough the term "vinárna" means wine bar in Czech, most of them function purely as estaurants.

WINE BARS

Slovácká Vícha, Michalská 511/6, Prague 1, 224 225 860

Moravský Archiv vín, Navrátilova 1421/11, Prague 1, 296 325 019

U Mecenáše, Malostranské nám. 261/10, Prague 1, 257 531 631

U krkavců, Dlouhá 735/25, Prague 1, 224 817 264

U císařů, Loretánská 175/5, Prague 1, 220 518 484

NIGHT CLUBS AND BARS

NIGHTCLUBS

Duplex, Václavské nám. 21, Prague 1, 224 232 319

Solidní Nejistota, Pštrossova 21, Prague 1, 224 933 086

Ultramarin, Ostrovní 32, Prague 1, 224 932 249

La Bodequita del Medio, Kaprova 5, Prague 1, 224 913 922

BARS

Tretter's, V Kolkovně 3, Prague 1, 224 811 165

Bugsy's, Pařížská 10, Prague 1, 224 810 287

Ocean Drive, V Kolkovně 7, Prague 1, 224 819 089

Well Tower of Karlštejn Castle.